BUILDERS OF
THE MILLENNIUM

A Series of Lectures
delivered to celebrate
the 750th Anniversary of
the Endowment of
University College, Oxford
1249–1999

University College, Oxford

Published by University College, Oxford 2000

First published 2000

The lecture by Sir V. S. Naipaul is based on his book
Reading and Writing: A Personal Account
and is reproduced here with his kind permission

Builders of the Millennium

ISBN 0-9539619-0-7

Printed in Great Britain by
Oxuniprint,
Oxford University Press

Foreword by

Lord Butler of Brockwell GCB, CVO

Master of University College, Oxford

When I took up my appointment as Master of University College in January 1998 twelve months before the College was due to begin the 750th anniversary of its endowment by William of Durham, the College had already decided to mount a series of lectures as part of the celebration.

It was envisaged that these lectures should be given by eminent people and should cover a wide range of the disciplines in which the College has been distinguished. It was also envisaged that they should be forward-looking, based on past associations where appropriate but focussing on the future.

I suggested that, given this specification, the theme of the lectures should be 'Builders of the Millennium'. The idea was that the College was beginning the last quarter of the first millennium of its recorded history and in the shorter term the world was about to begin the third millennium of the Christian era. With this title we hoped to attract the movers and shakers who were shaping the world at the opening of the coming century.

Given the College's association with Lord Beveridge's 1942 report, drafted while Beveridge was Master of Univ., the future of the welfare state at the beginning of the 21st century was a natural subject to open the series and we were privileged that the Prime Minister himself agreed to give this lecture. It was also appropriate that he should have given it at Toynbee Hall, so closely linked with both Beveridge and Attlee, our first Univ. Prime Minister. The Prime Minister's speech was an important one—not only his first major statement in office on the future of the welfare state but also the speech in which he first announced the Government's target of ending child poverty in 20 years.

Our next two speakers were eminent Continental Europeans, with leading positions in two areas of prime importance on the threshold of the new millennium—Professor Hans Tietmeyer, President of the Deutsche Bundesbank, who spoke about the Euro and economic convergence, and the President of the Italian Chamber of Deputies, Luciano Violante, former Investigating Magistrate at Turin, with an heroic record against the Red Brigade and the Mafia, who spoke about progress in combatting organised crime.

In the fields of science and literature we were delighted that the College's alumni, Professor Stephen Hawking and Sir V.S. Naipaul, agreed to participate. We could not have had two more celebrated speakers in these two fields, and they are the College's own. They symbolised the scholarly peaks the College has achieved in science and literature.

The two final speakers in the series were Sir Richard Branson and Rupert Murdoch, leading figures in enterprise and media. These pursuits are undeniably important in shaping life at the start of the third millennium. It is difficult to avoid reflecting how astonished William of Durham would be that the 750th anniversary of his benefaction should be celebrated with lectures on such subjects.

In addition to the Toynbee Hall setting of the Prime Minister's lecture, Oxford provided some of its noblest settings for the other lectures in the series—the Sheldonian, the Examination Schools, Oxford Town Hall and the Old Library at All Souls. These made each occasion a memorable one. We are grateful to the University and City authorities for making these magnificent settings available.

So this book brings together seven different contributions on aspects of life at the beginning of the third millennium, all from very distinguished leaders in their fields. The College is grateful to all our lecturers, to Mrs. Biddy Hayward for her organisation of the events, and to the College Archivist, Dr. Robin Darwall-Smith, for his meticulous editing of the texts and transcripts. We are also very grateful to the Prudential Corporation who sponsored the lecture series. We hope that this booklet will present a useful statement about issues and attitudes at the beginning of the 21st century and be an appropriate token of the position the College has achieved in the 750 years of its life since William of Durham's endowment.

CONTENTS

THE LECTURERS

THE RT. HON. TONY BLAIR, MP, was born in 1953, He attended St. John's College, Oxford, and was called to the bar at Lincoln's Inn in 1976, of which he became an Honorary Bencher in 1994. In 1983 he was elected Labour MP for Sedgefield. In the Shadow Cabinet, he served as Shadow Home Secretary, and in 1994 was elected leader of the Labour Party, being appointed a Privy Councillor in the same year. From 1994–1997 he was Leader of the Opposition. After his party's victory in the General Election of May 1997, Tony Blair became Prime Minister of the United Kingdom.

PROFESSOR LUCIANO VIOLANTE was born in 1941. He read Law at Bari University, and became a Professor of Public Law there from 1974–1981, and in 1983 a Professor of Criminal Law and Procedure. He had also been a magistrate since 1966, acting as Investigating Magistrate at Turin until 1977, and in 1977–1979 worked for the Ministry of Justice, with special responsibilities for the fight against terrorism. In 1979 he became a Member of Parliament, where he was a member of several committees relating to criminal matters, including the Commission on the Aldo Moro case and the Commission for the reform of the Criminal Code. In 1992–1994 he served as Chairman of the Anti-Mafia Committee, and in 1994–1996 as Vice-President of the Chamber of Deputies, of which he was elected President in 1996. Professor Violante has also written extensively on legal and criminal matters.

PROFESSOR DR. DR. H. C. HANS TIETMEYER was born in 1931. He studied economics and social sciences at the Universities of Münster, Bonn and Cologne, before gaining a Doctorate in economics in 1960. From 1962–1982, he worked at the Federal Ministry of Economics, becoming Head of the Directorate-General responsible for economic policy in 1973. In 1982 he became Permanent Secretary at the Federal Ministry of Finance with particular responsibility for international monetary policy, EC matters and the preparation of World Economic Summits. In 1990 Professor Tietmeyer was appointed to the Board of the Deutsche Bundesbank, and of the Central Bank Council. In 1993 he was appointed President of the Deutsche Bundesbank and in 1994 he became Chairman of the G-10 Central Bank of Governors. He has also been Chairman of such international bodies as the EC Economic Policy Committee and the EC Monetary Committee. Professor Tietmeyer has received honorary doctorates from several universities, as well as the Grand Cross of the Order of Merit of the Federal Republic of Germany.

PROFESSOR STEPHEN HAWKING, CH, CBE, FRS was born in 1942, and went to University College (his father's old College), where he was awarded a First in Natural Science before going on to Cambridge to research Cosmology. After gaining his Ph.D. he became a Research Fellow, and then a Professorial Fellow at Gonville and Caius College. Since 1969 he has held the post of Lucasian Professor of Mathematics, a chair previously held by Isaac Newton. Stephen Hawking is perhaps best known for his discovery, in 1974, that black holes emit radiation, and for his no boundary proposal made in 1983 with Jim Hartle of Santa Barbara. His many publications include two popular books: his best seller *A Brief History of Time*, and his later book, *Black Holes and Baby Universes and Other Essays*. Professor Hawking is a Fellow of the Royal Society and a Member of the US National Academy of Sciences, has twelve honorary degrees, and is the recipient of many awards, medals and prizes. He was awarded the CBE in 1982 and was made a Companion of Honour in 1989.

SIR RICHARD BRANSON was born in 1950. He began his business career at school, where at the age of 16 he established a national magazine called *Student*. In 1970 he founded Virgin as a mail order record retailer and soon opened a record shop in Oxford Street. The first Virgin artist, Mike Oldfield, recorded 'Tubular Bells' in 1972, which helped make Virgin Music one of the top six record companies in the world. In 1984, Sir Richard founded Virgin Atlantic Airways, and the interests of his Virgin Group now encompass the 'Megastore' music retailing chain, the Internet, book and software publishing, film and video editing facilities, clubs, travel, hotels and cinemas through over 100 companies in 23 countries. In addition to his business activities, Sir Richard is also a trustee of several charities, and in 1986 he captained the *Atlantic Challenger II*, which won the Blue Riband for the fastest crossing of the Atlantic, and in 1987 and 1991 respectively led the teams which flew the first hot air balloons to cross the Atlantic and the Pacific. Richard Branson was knighted in 2000.

SIR VIDIADHAR (V. S.) NAIPAUL was born, of Indian ancestry, in Trinidad in 1932. He came to England in 1950. He studied at University College and began to write, in London, in 1954. He has pursued no other profession. His works of fiction include *A House for Mr. Biswas*, *Mr Stone and the Knight's Companion* (Hawthornden Prize), *The Mimic Men* (W.H. Smith Award), *In a Free State* (Booker Prize) and, most recently, *A Way in the World* (1994). In 1960 he began to travel and his travel writings include *An Area of Darkness, India: A Wounded Civilization* and *India: A Million Mutinies Now* (which together form his *Indian Trilogy*), *The Loss of El Dorado*, a study of New World history, *The Return of Eva Peron* (with *The Killings in Trinidad*), based on travels in Argentina, Trinidad and the Congo, and *Among the Believers: An Islamic Journey*. In 1995 he returned to Indonesia, Iran, Pakistan and Malaysia. *Beyond Belief*, his account of those travels, was published in 1998. V.S. Naipaul received a knighthood in the 1990 New Year's Honours List for services to literature; in 1993 he was the first recipient of the David Cohen British Literature Prize.

RUPERT MURDOCH AC was born in Melbourne, Australia, in 1931. He graduated from Oxford in 1953 and, after working at the *Daily Express* in London, returned to Australia. In 1954 he took control of News Limited. After acquiring and launching several Australian papers, he acquired *News of the World* in 1969, and later *The Sun* newspaper. In the 1980s the company purchased *The Times, The Sunday Times* and book publisher HarperCollins. Mr. Murdoch is now the Chairman and Chief Executive of News Corporation Limited, whose global operations include newspaper and magazine publishing on three continents; significant book publishing interests; major film and television production and distribution operations; and television, satellite and cable broadcast operations throughout the world, including British Sky Broadcasting, the UK's first satellite broadcasting operation. It also purchased Twentieth Century Fox Film Corporation in 1985. Mr. Murdoch and his family have always been closely involved with, and made generous contributions to, various charitable organisations. In 1984 Mr. Murdoch was awarded the Companion of the Order of Australia (AC) for services to the media and to newspaper publishing in particular.

BEVERIDGE REVISITED: A WELFARE STATE FOR THE 21ST CENTURY

By

THE RT. HON TONY BLAIR, MP

A lecture delivered at
Toynbee Hall, London,
on 18 March 1999

1

Iam delighted to play my part in celebrating the remarkable anniversary of University College which takes place this year.

There is a close connection between Toynbee Hall and Oxford University. The decision to found this settlement was taken in 1883 at Balliol, the neighbour of my own College of St. John's. In the same year William Morris scandalised the then Master of University College through a speech in the College canvassing support for the socialist movement. No doubt the present Master would have handled things differently.

Second, there is the connection with University College. It is a remarkable coincidence that both William Beveridge, a young don at University College in the early years of the century, and Clement Attlee, an undergraduate there, spent some of their early years here at Toynbee Hall and subsequently both played such a major role in the formation of the post-war welfare state—again, in Beveridge's case, at University College.

If I may say just one word of thanks to Robin personally, I am also delighted to be his guest. As Cabinet Secretary, he was extremely kind to me when we won the election on May 1997. I shall never forget that time: straight after you win the election, then you go to the Palace and you come into No. 10 Downing Street. With this great tradition we have in Britain, you go straight in—it's not like the States when you have three or four months to prepare. I remember walking down the corridor of Downing Street for only the second time in my life and then meeting Robin in a little room just off the Cabinet Room, and he said to me, 'Well, you're in charge. What are we going to do, then?' One of the more alarming opening remarks I've ever encountered. I won't tell you what I replied. But it's worth recording for him personally that he did, I think, a remarkable job in the transition. After 18 years of one party in government, to come in with another party and to govern was in part a remarkable tribute to the Civil Service and obviously to the leadership that he showed as Cabinet Secretary.

* * *

Today I want to talk to you about a great challenge: how we make the welfare state popular again. How we restore public trust and confidence in a welfare state that fifty years ago was acclaimed but today has so many wanting to bury it. I will argue that the only road to 'a popular welfare state' is radical welfare reform. And I will set out our historic aim that ours should be the first generation to end child poverty for ever, and it will take a generation. It is a twenty year mission but I believe it can be done.

3

It is worth recapping briefly on the enormous amount of reform now under way. Partly because the Opposition aren't quite sure what to say about it, it has been less controversial than many anticipated. But those who predicted timidity have been proven wholly wrong. In two years we have:

- reformed the whole of student finance;
- introduced the largest programme for the young unemployed ever put in place in Britain;
- published, and are now legislating, the Welfare Reform Bill that will modernise the whole of disability provision, benefit claims and support in bereavement, and introduce stakeholder pensions;
- set out a framework for future pension reform that will alter the entirety of pension provision over the next twenty years, whilst introducing the Minimum Income Guarantee for today's pensioners;
- made radical proposals to reform the Child Support Agency and the whole of legal aid;
- and of course, we are changing through the Working Family Tax Credit, the new family credit and 20% increase in Child Benefit, the whole of provision for children and for families.

And we are now turning our attention to long-term care and housing benefit. It is the fullest programme of reform of any Government this century. Certainly it ranks alongside the Liberal Government of 1906 and the Labour Government of 1945. And I believe it is wholly in the spirit of Beveridge.

Beveridge was perhaps the greatest British social reformer of the 20th century. He was a brilliant but difficult man. He devoted his life to understanding and abolishing poverty starting here at Toynbee Hall. He was a remarkable talent and enthusiast. Permanent Secretary at 39. And able to say at 80 that 'I am still radical and young enough to believe that mountains can be moved'. He was in the Liberal party but really a forerunner of modern social democracy, arguing for top class public services for all. When people ask me why I favour stronger links between Labour and the Liberal Democrats, I say and mean that my lexicon of political heroes include Keynes and Beveridge, alongside Keir Hardie, Bevan and Attlee.

Beveridge laid the foundations of the modern welfare state. His plan, published in 1942, heralded the first British comprehensive system of free health care; universal family support; and rights to minimum rates of social insurance benefits during old age or in the event of unemployment, sickness or disability. It transformed Britain for the better. It improved the health of the nation and in large measure removed absolute poverty and destitution from our country. It was an enormous step change, ending the lottery of state welfare that had existed since the Poor Law.

But, as Tony Atkinson has said, Beveridge would have been 'profoundly irritated' by any assumption that his plan could serve the needs of the 21st century as well as it has served the 20th century. His views were constantly evolving, constantly changing to meet new needs.

* * *

Social justice is as relevant today as it was for Beveridge. It is the aim of this New Labour Government. It is our central belief—the basis for a community where everyone has the chance to succeed.

Social justice is about decency. It requires that any citizen of our society should be able to meet their needs for income, housing, health and education.

Social justice is about merit rather than privilege. It demands that life chances should depend on talent and effort, not the chance of birth; and that talent and effort should be handsomely rewarded. The child born on a run-down housing estate should have the same chance to be healthy and well educated as the child born in the leafy suburbs. Indeed it is only when you put it like that you see the distance we have to go.

Social justice is about mutual responsibility. It insists that we all accept duties as well as rights—to each other and to society.

Social justice is about fairness. In a community founded on social justice, power, wealth and opportunity will be the hands of the many not the few. These words come from the new Clause 4 of the Labour Party constitution and they are what New Labour is about.

Social justice is about values. The values are timeless. But their application must change with changing times. That is why it is New Labour.

As John Hills has written, Beveridge's plan for the 'abolition of want' was based on his reading of research on the nature of poverty and society in the 1930s. His solution was tailored to fit the needs of the day. In the last sixty years the world has changed dramatically. It would be surprising, lazy even, to believe that the solutions that suited a post-war Britain could work just as well in today's global economy.

Most strikingly the position of women has changed. Beveridge drew on the 1931 census to argue that:

'More that seven out of eight of all housewives, that is to say married women of working age, made marriage their sole occupation; less than one in eight of all housewives was also gainfully occupied.'

He assumed that after the war, when women had worked in far greater numbers, that the world would remain the same. But it didn't. Sixty years on women's lives have been transformed. Half the workforce today is made up of women. And Beveridge would have been amazed that one in five of all families with children was headed by a lone parent.

Our society has aged. This would have surprised Beveridge less. Only 10% of the population was over state pension age in 1931. In 1991 it was 18%. In 2021 it will be 21%. And while there is no 'demographic timebomb' in Britain, as some would have us believe, we have gradually become an older population.

Work patterns have changed. Beveridge like most of his contemporaries, was committed to full employment, delivered by Keynesian demand management.

The assumption of enduring full employment held good during the 1940s and 1950s when jobs were plentiful thanks to post war reconstruction. It didn't matter so much how poorly skilled people were. Work was easy to come by, though in the main, of course, it was the men who worked. That assumption began to come apart as early as the 1970s when traditional demand management failed to curb rising unemployment.

Today the assumption has completely broken down. Globalisation has placed a premium on workers with the skills and knowledge to adapt to advancing technology. People without skills find it very hard to compete. If they can find work it is too often short term and so poorly paid that it does not provide a springboard out of poverty. New groups of unemployed have appeared: people taking early retirement because of incapacity and parents bringing up young children on their own.

By the 1970s it was plain that the welfare state of the first half of the 20th century wasn't going to be right for the second half of the 20th century. One of the key insights of Beveridge was his fundamental belief that the concept of social welfare had to fit economic policy. He fashioned the welfare stare around a view of the economy—the full employment, mass production economy of the 1940s.

By the 1970s, economic policy and social policy were becoming divorced. Welfare policy—redistribution, social security—were seen almost as antithetical to sound economic policy. The welfare state was in certain quarters being seen as a burden to be paid for at the expense of wealth creation.

The left at that time, trapped in a false confusion of means and ends, resisted changing the welfare state on the grounds that to modernise the welfare state, was somehow to undermine it. Social justice became, on the left, identified with rigid policy prescriptions, good for the 1940's increasingly out of date for the 1970's. The right moved in.

* * *

I asked David Piachaud to write a paper in preparation for this speech. As he points out, after eighteen years of Conservative government there was:

- more poverty—one third of children living in families under half average income levels;
- more inequality between rich and poor;
- more dependence on benefits, particularly means tested benefits;
- more homeless on the streets.

The right came to power, committed to cutting welfare costs. The fundamental irony is it ended up in increasing them. No budget of any department rose more under the last government than Social Security. This was despite many measures—like ending the link between earnings and pensions—which cut costs.

The reason is simple. Whereas the old left regarded the application of social justice as something to remain unchanged, the right regarded it as irrelevant. They believed it didn't matter; and that it had no connection with economic efficiency. Indeed, it is that curious alliance of the right and old left that I have witnessed and struggled against all my political life, for both left and right agreed to divorce economic efficiency from social justice. Both saw wealth creation as in opposition to social justice. You had to choose between one or the other.

The right were mistaken about the importance of markets and greater competition. But they failed to see in the modern world, that it is not enough. Indeed perhaps it was never enough.

Keynes wrote of this flawed approach.

'The Economists were teaching that wealth, commerce and machinery were the children of free competition ... But the Darwinians could go one better than that—free competition had built Man. The human eye was no longer the demonstration of [God's] design, miraculously contriving all things for the best; it was the supreme achievement of Chance, operating under conditions of free competition and laissez-faire. The principle of the Survival of the Fittest could be regarded as a vast generalisation of Ricardian economics. Socialistic interferences became, in the light of this grander synthesis, not merely inexpedient, but impious, as calculated to retard the onward movement of the mighty process by which we ourselves had risen like Aphrodite out of the primeval slime of the Ocean.'

So under the last Government, social security spending went up, but poverty and social exclusion went up too. So they cut away at the Budget, sometimes creating problems along the way—for example, encouraging fraud in their cuts to housing benefit. But they failed to tackle the fundamental weaknesses of the welfare state. They left unreformed areas that had become outdated such as the inadequacy of childcare support for working women. They failed to create a modern welfare state fit for the modern world.

But in the process, with the left trying to defend an unreformed welfare state, and the right chipping away at it and in the process not succeeding, welfare became unpopular. Welfare, though not the concept of the welfare state, became a term of abuse. It became associated with fraud, abuse, laziness, a dependency culture, social irresponsibility encouraged by welfare dependency. Welfare was blamed as the problem not the solution.

This, if we define welfare as the welfare state, is dangerous.

For if people lose faith in the welfare state's ability to deliver, then politicians have an impossible job persuading hard pressed taxpayers that their money should go on a system that is not working. If all welfare—the good spending as well as the bad—becomes stigmatised then the security of children, the disabled, pensioners is put at risk

The Welfare State was popular in Beveridge's day, because Beveridge made it popular. It was associated with progress and achievement. Providing people with their first pension, a decent home, peace of mind when unemployed. Our job is to make the welfare state once again a force for progress. I want to make all of the welfare state as popular as the NHS because it is providing real security and opportunity, because we have rooted out fraud and because we are giving greatest help to those with the greatest needs.

* * *

The third way in welfare is clear: not to dismantle it; or to protect it unchanged; but to reform it radically—taking its core values and applying them afresh to the modern world.

Above all, we must reconnect social justice to economic vision. Our economic vision for Britain in the 21st century is clear: stability in economic management; and then, on that foundation, the building of the knowledge economy, where we compete by skill, talent and technology. Education is an economic as well as a social imperative. In the Green Paper on welfare, published last March, we called for a new welfare contract between the citizens of the country based on the principle 'Work for those who can work; security for those who can't'. This means refocusing dramatically the objectives and operation of the welfare state. If the knowledge economy is our aim, then work, skill and, above all, investing in children, become essential aims of the welfare state. Of course, security for those who can't work or are retired is vital; and big change is needed there too. But a welfare state that is just about 'social security' is inadequate. It is passive where we now need it to be active. It encourages dependency where in fact we need it to encourage independence, initiative, enterprise for all.

By linking it to an economic vision, the welfare state, radically reformed, can be popular because everyone, haves and have nots, can not see just its raison d'etre, but can also understand why it is in their interests to support and sustain it.

The characteristic of the modern popular welfare state will, in my judgement, be the following:

First, it has to tackle social exclusion, child poverty, community decay in an active way; and tackle it through tackling the fundamental causes: structural unemployment; poor education; poor housing; the crime and drugs culture. The talent we waste through social exclusion, we waste not just for the individual but for the nation. Let us liberate it and use it for the nation.

Second, welfare will be a hand-up not a hand-out. Mutual responsibility. We have a responsibility to provide young people with life chances. They have a responsibility to take them. Parents have responsibility for their children. Those who can do so have a responsibility to save for their retirement. The state becomes an enabler, not just a provider. Otherwise the costs are out of control and the consent for the taxpayer to fund welfare declines.

Third, where people really need security, the most help should go to those with the most need. There will always be a mix of universal and targeted help. But the one is not 'superior' or 'more principled' than the other.

Fourth, we must root out fraud and abuse in any way we can and, as Frank Field has rightly said, not just in individual cases, but by ending the systemic encouragement of fraud in the way the welfare state is designed.

Fifth, the welfare state need no longer be delivered only through the state or through traditional methods of Government. Public/private partnership and the voluntary sector will have and should have a greater role to play.

Sixth, the welfare state cannot not just be about benefits. Active welfare is about services too—schools, hospitals, the whole infrastructure of community support.

* * *

So that's the vision for a popular welfare state. What are we doing to make it happen? At every level, we are implementing it.

We are getting people back into work. The New Deal embodies the new ethic at the heart of our reforms—mutual responsibilities. It means government offering real opportunities, but people having an obligation to take them or risk losing benefits. 230,000 young people have already joined the programme and 60,000 are already in jobs. Since we took office long term unemployment among young people has halved and the combination of sound economic policies and active policies in the labour market mean that Britain has now created net nearly half a million new jobs, a huge advance in opportunities. And we have extended the New Deal from the young unemployed to lone parents, the disabled who want to work and to the over-50s. To make the system work better we are introducing what we call a 'single gateway' into the welfare system for all benefit claimants of working age. That means personalised help for people but a requirement they attend interviews.

Despite some carping from the usual suspects, the new deal is an extraordinary success. 40,000 employers are signed up. Their biggest complaint is they can't get enough of the New Dealers. The New Dealers' biggest complaint is trying to get on the New Deal. To the cynics, I say: talk to the young people and the lone parents, thousands of them now in work. The New Deal is no YTS; no skivvy scheme. It is empowerment in action and I am proud of it.

We are making work pay. The Working Families Tax Credit, the minimum wage, the childcare credit will make work pay for millions of families. Our deal: if you work hard you will not be in poverty. Our guarantee: that if you work full time you will take home at least £10,000 a year and you will not have to pay any tax until you earn £12,500 a year. On April 1 this government will introduce Britain's first ever minimum wage. This will be a great landmark for the country. A symbol of fairness. An act of social justice that Beveridge would have been proud to call his own.

We are modernising public services. We are not just putting an extra 40 billion pounds of additional investment into schools and hospitals over the next three years; we are insisting that it is tied to modernisation and change. In education we are taking the action needed to turn round our schools so that every parent can rely on a decent education for their children. We are focussing on literacy and numeracy; better pay, recognition and status for teachers; a relentless attack on failure wherever it occurs. In health we are trying to turn a treasured but often unresponsive health service into a modern, consumer focussed, quality NHS through modern building and equipment, modernised primary care services, proper quality audit and faster care. In education and health it is not just money going in; at every step of the way it is tied to radical change in reform and modernisation.

We are tackling social decay. 800 million pounds in the New Deal for Communities to turn around our poorest housing estates. Action is being taken in London and other cities to ensure that no-one has to sleep rough on the streets. Measures to stop the truancy and exclusions that mean that thousands leave school without any qualifications. And in each of these areas we are bringing the different parts of government to work together. This is all about preventing tomorrow's problems rather than only picking up the pieces from missed opportunities in the past. We are bringing hope to communities that had lost hope. We are fostering local and community innovation. Local people often know best what they need and how to provide it.

I asked Bob Holman who is a community worker and sociology professor in Glasgow what he thought. He told me of one neighbourhood project in Easterhouse. A woman who started to help out at a local lunch club then became a member of the local co-operative eventually becoming its chair. As her self confidence grew she was able again to take custody of her child that had been taken away from her, and is now a respected community activist. It is stories like these that can happen day in day out if the help and the infrastructure is provided there.

We are proving real security for those who can't work or have retired. Severely disabled people with the greatest needs will get a significant increase in income. Pensioners are now benefiting from a guaranteed income that will go up in line with earnings not just prices. Free eye tests are being restored from April. And we are raising the winter allowance to £100 so that today's pensioners can benefit. Real security for those most in need, but at the same time a dramatic change in the way that we fund and deliver pension provision for the future.

And in doing so we are building new public and private partnerships. There needs to be a mixed economy in the funding of welfare comprising the state, private and voluntary sectors. In pensions we are shifting the balance of funding from the state to the private sector. Currently funding is split 60% state, 40% private. This will reverse to 40% state, 60% private, as the less well off take up the new stakeholder pensions.

But we are also developing mixed partnerships in the delivery of other parts of welfare. We have made a start in the new deal involving the private providers, the voluntary sector, parents and we intend to go further.

So all these areas change in being implemented, but above all our welfare reform programme will give children—all children—the support they need. Our approach on children brings together all the lessons we have learned from applying reform in other areas.

We have made children our top priority because as the Chancellor memorably said in his Budget 'they are 20% of the population but they are 100% of the future'.

The levels of child deprivation are still frightening:

- almost one in three children in our country lives in poverty;
- poor children are two and a half times more likely to have no qualifications;
- girls from deprived backgrounds are ten times more likely to have a teenage pregnancy than girls from well off families;
- poor children are more likely to play truant;
- more likely to get excluded from school;
- more likely to get in trouble with the police;
- more likely to live in a deprived area;
- more likely to be from an ethnic minority family;
- more likely to be brought up by one parent.

And in the last 20 years the tax burden on ordinary families has increased. At the very time that families have come under increasing pressure, juggling work and home, the state has made it harder than ever for them to cope.

We need to break the cycle of disadvantage so that children born into poverty are not condemned to social exclusion and deprivation. That is why it is so important that we invest in our children.

But our reforms will help more than the poorest children. All parents need help. All children need support.

Across Government, children are getting a better deal. Our family policy is geared to children and their well being more than the type of family that child is born to. I make no apologies for that. Education is our number one priority precisely because without skills and knowledge children will not succeed in life. And our welfare policy, therefore, does all that it can to lift children out of poverty at key points in their lives.

Throughout their childhood we are introducing a wholly new system at virtually every level to give children the support they need.

At birth, families are getting more child benefit, a new children's tax credit and extended maternity support.

In the early years, we want all parents to have the chance to spend more time with their children. So we have introduced new rights to parental leave. We want children to be ready to learn when they start school. So we are expanding childcare and nursery care, with a special Sure Start programme for children at particular risk of social exclusion. These new services will also help parents who wish to return to work, supported by the working families tax credit and the minimum wage.

In their school years, we want our children to have the best education possible. That is why we're driving up school standards, tackling failing schools, concentrating on giving children the basic skills of reading, writing and numeracy that they need to get on. But we also want them to have worthwhile activities to go to outside school. There is nothing more dispiriting than seeing a thirteen-year-old hanging around on the streets with nothing to do. That's why we're bringing in a national network of after school clubs providing opportunities to learn and play.

The cumulative effect of the proposals we've introduced over this two year period will be that we will lift 700,000 children out of poverty by the end of the Parliament. Poverty should not be a birthright. Being poor should not be a life sentence. We need to sow the seeds of ambition in the young.

Our historic aim will be for ours to be the first generation to end child poverty, and it will take a generation. It is a twenty year mission but I believe it can be done, if we reform the welfare state and build it around the needs of families and children.

* * *

The consequence of these reforms is a quiet revolution. They are being carried through by a quiet revolutionary—Alistair Darling.

We are already beginning to see the results. The messages we send into the system about the importance of work do bear fruit. Since we came to government we have cut the real growth of social security spending by almost one per cent a year. In our first two years we have spent over five billion pounds less than the previous Government planned for.

In the future we will increase provision on our priority areas—children, pensioners, disabled people. So we are keeping our promise to cut the bills of social and economic failure, whilst spending more on education, the NHS and those in our welfare state who really need help.

The prize for us is to have welfare spending under control; to have good spending on areas we want money spent on—like child benefit and pensions—going up. Bad spending on the bills of economic failure is coming down.

Spending this Parliament on children will increase by more than six billion pounds, but at the same time by the New Deal, by the measures we are taking to tackle social exclusion, we will manage to get the bills of social and economic failure down.

We are creating a welfare system which is 'active' not 'passive', genuinely providing people with a 'hand up' not a 'hand out'. Previous governments were satisfied simply to dole out money. The Tories spent over 90 billion pounds on benefits, but a fraction of that sum on getting people back to work. The radical reforms of the welfare state that we are proposing change that around. We believe that the role of the welfare state is to help people help themselves, to give people the means to be independent. that is precisely why we are creating an active welfare state focussed on giving people the opportunities they need to support themselves, principally through work.

* * *

These, therefore, are the changes that we have implemented, and in my lecture to you I have tried to track the enormous social changes that have happened and how that should be reflected in a different vision of the welfare statute for the future, and tried to link that to the specific programmes which the government is carrying through.

I believe Beveridge would have been proud of the changes we are making. The aims have not changed since his day, but the means are radically reformed. I would go further. I would like to think that he and Keynes would have been proud to be supporters of New Labour or at least let us say on the co-operative wing of the Liberal Democrats! Both are part of the heritage that today's Labour Party draws upon. That is because the Labour Party has, through New Labour, returned to our roots, which were always about values. At its best, the centre-left of politics—and here I include people outside my Party as well as in it—has stood for two things, progress and justice. To be the advocates of the future with fairness. Modernising always, but for a purpose: to build a better, fairer, society, where economic prosperity and social justice go hand and hand and where, as the new Clause IV says, we live together freely in a spirit of solidarity, tolerance and respect. If we fail to have that purpose, of creating that type of country and society for the future, then we fail to have a purpose worthy of our political ambition. But if on the other hand we fail constantly to modernise and update the application of these values to the world in which we live, then we cease to become a movement for change and merely become a political monument.

A modern popular welfare state is an integral part of a bigger picture. The vision for Britain under New Labour is very simply summarised:

- a modern economy based on stability and knowledge;
- a modern civic society based n a reformed welfare state;
- a modern constitution which gives more power to the people;
- a modern approach to the world in which Britain loses its post-Empire lack of confidence and reaches out strong and engaged to play its full part in Europe and the wider world.

I believe that that vision is within our grasp. As the 21st century beckons, it is time to make that vision and the modern popular welfare state that at its heart, a reality for us and for future generations.

THE FIGHT AGAINST CORRUPTION AND ORGANISED CRIME UNDER THE RULE OF LAW

By

Prof. Luciano Violante

The H.L.A. Hart Memorial Lecture for 1999
delivered at All Souls College, Oxford,
on 1 June 1999

Allow me to start by thanking you for your invitation to participate in this cycle of Lectures. I am especially honoured to address this distinguished gathering at the prestigious University of Oxford.

I have divided my paper into four parts: a) the main features of organised crime; b) corruption; c) the main features of the fight against organised crime and corruption; d) education to foster respect for the law.

Before addressing the first issue, the features of organised crime, allow me to clarify two points.

The first is the difference between mafia and organised crime. Mafia is that particular form of organised crime that has relations with politics and that uses these relations to do business and to secure its immunity. While mafia certainly is a form of organised crime, not all organised crime is mafia, because not all organised crime has a relationship with politics.

The second point is a little longer: it deals with the difference between 'international organised crime' and 'transnational organised crime'. The two expressions are often used interchangeably but they indicate different situations, although they have some points in common.

The term international means that the members of criminal organisations of different countries may be operating together within the same structure.

The term transnational defines the operational capacity of criminal organisations across the borders of many countries.

* * *

I will now analyse the concepts of international and transnational crime.

Internationalisation has expanded since the sixties, owing to the growth in the trade of the commodities in which organised crime deals: arms and drugs. Both are consumed in places other than where they are produced. Shipments of drugs and arms must cross many countries before they reach the country where they will be used. Dealers in these products have to cross national borders, make use of legitimate institutions (such as banks, holding companies and customs authorities) and maintain relations with criminal groups in various countries. This form of trade has generated strong international relations amongst all of the most dangerous criminal organisations.

The traditional markets of organised crime—drugs and arms—have been flanked by a third market: the trafficking in human beings. These people may be refugees from war- torn regions, immigrants seeking employment, which they cannot find in their own country, or women and children trapped in the web of prostitution.

This trafficking in human beings is our modern-day version of the old slave trade. The UN has estimated the income of trafficking in human beings at around 5 billion dollars. Between the fourteenth and seventeenth centuries, the slavery involved 12 million people. Today, in all the world, there are 200 million people in conditions of slavery.

The use of children is a new development: most child trafficking aims at recruiting children for menial tasks within criminal bands, such as the transport of weapons, the street-side distribution of drugs and watching over prostitutes. Then there is paedophilia which accounts for a small, albeit a horrible, share of this market.

Modern criminal organisations have a strong interest in cost reduction and risk avoidance. Children are ideal for this purpose. It is easy for children to pass unnoticed and they are also less likely to be believed by authorities if they make any accusations to the police. Last but not least children keep costs down because they are content with very little.

I will now move on to the transnational dimension, which does not describe the make-up of the criminal organisations, but rather their field of action. Transnational criminal organisations put their men, headquarters and businesses in different countries, according to factors such as the return on investments, the stringency of controls and the potential for expansion .

The transnational dimension is due to the changing geo-strategic conditions world-wide. Market globalisation after the collapse of the Soviet system has resulted in the movement of money, goods and people at a speed and with an ease that would have been simply unthinkable in the past.

Honest citizens travel the world with ease. But so do the members of the major criminal organisations. And it is often so hard to tell these people apart: they dress alike and speak alike, they move in similar social circles and dine in the same restaurants. The fact that only about three per cent of the nine million containers that enter the USA annually are checked by U.S. Customs underscores the problem.

The second trend, besides globalisation, that was started by the end of the Soviet system was the transition to democracy of many former Communist countries. The process of democratic transition has opened up very good opportunities for organised crime. In some of these countries the State is often still unprepared to govern the transition process. In a transition, institutions are fragile, money is scarce and so are consumer goods. Also, the citizens of these countries, owing to their unhappy past experiences in the police-State under the Soviet regime, have a deep-seated distrust towards police measures. A weak state, a weak market and a lack of respect for the law have created the ideal conditions for the entry of organised crime.

If you imagine a geographical map of crime, Central Europe is surrounded by the Russian mafia to the East, by the Turkish and Albanian mafias to the South East and by the Italian mafia to the West. It is like a nut squeezed in a giant nutcracker.

About eighty per cent of the heroin consumed in Europe is shipped via the Balkan routes. The war, and the resulting destabilisation, have contributed to reinforce the criminal groups that have their interests in this area.

In conclusion, Central Europe is an area of transit and criminal investment. But with its 245 million inhabitants and a GDP of 1,450 billion dollars, it may easily turn into a huge market for organised crime.

Central Europe may well become the 'back-yard' of the Italian, Russian, Turkish and Albanian mafias, who would create alliances with local crime and thus establish a geo-criminal area.

For most governments of Central Europe combatting organised crime is a leading national priority. But many still do not have the laws and regulations, the facilities and professional expertise to achieve effective control. These countries must be helped—that is in our own interest.

So far we have described the make-up of the major criminal organisations and their geographical sphere of action. Let us now move on to the main operational features of organised crime.

The following list of features of international and transnational organisations—which I am now going to illustrate—is not the result of a purely academic exercise. It is based on our experience. They are what we should look for when examining the conduct of suspects to establish whether they belong to organised criminal groups.

(1) Their professional mission is to achieve the greatest possible wealth with the highest possible degree of immunity.

(2) They engage in every type of illegal, or apparently legal profit-generating activity: for example mafia expert Alison Jamieson reports that the Sicilian Cuntrera Caruana clan maintains a wine bar, an antiques business and a travel agency in the U.K. as cover for importation of cannabis from Kashmir and heroin from Thailand.

(3) Their main tools are intimidation, corruption, violence.

(4) They have rigid internal hierarchies and fierce sanctioning systems based on the physical elimination of anyone who has seriously harmed the organisation or is suspected of having done so in the past, or of being capable of doing so in the future.

(5) They benefit from a high-level network of professional expertise in financial, legal and trade matters.

(6) They try to infiltrate the government institutions, the police, the judiciary, political bodies, ministries and local government in every possible way.

(7) They entertain business relations with all other criminal organisations, and also with lawful organisations, to increase their profits, secure immunity and steadily expand their businesses.

(8) They are always seeking a legal umbrella, and therefore attempt to enter into financial, entrepreneurial and political circles.

(9) They aim at securing financial and entrepreneurial power.

(10) They are not interested in directly holding political power, as this might lead to excessive exposure. Rather, they make use of the political power in the hands of others.

Current estimates on the size of the criminal economy are far from certain because the proceeds are largely hidden. The figures put forward by the International Monetary Fund may be taken as a good indication. In a 1996 study, the IMF estimated the annual income of criminal organisations—which we may call the GCP, the Gross Criminal Product—at around 500 billion dollars, roughly equal to two per cent of the global GDP. This figure was forecast to double in the years following 1996. And may indeed have done so.

According to the latest United Nations report, 400 billion dollars of this income is generated by drug trafficking, which accounts for some eight per cent of the world's legal trade as a whole.

* * *

I will now move on to the second part of my presentation, the relations between organised crime and corruption. For groups that have a lot of money, corruption is a low-cost, low-risk and highly-effective tool.

Organised crime, if possible, chooses corruption, not murder. It only kills when it is absolutely necessary to do so. Because, while murder eliminates an obstacle, corruption creates an accomplice. A corrupt person in an institution is a door which is always open for criminal organisations. Corruption eliminates competition in the market, in contracts and in the administration of public services. It eliminates controls against illegal activities, such as drug trafficking or the exploitation of prostitution.

There is a difference between ordinary corruption and corruption as used by organised crime. Ordinary corruption tries to obtain a given favour from a civil servant. Corruption, as used by organised crime aims at binding a civil servant to crime. In the former, what is at stake is a favour. In the latter, a person's loyalty.

The bosses of organised crime know that soon or later they will need a police officer, a judge, an employee of the Finance Ministry, and so on. So they try to establish a relationship with that person. They start with little acts of courtesy, and then the gifts gradually become more and more valuable. When the occasion arises, the generous donor asks for the favour he needs and at that point it is very difficult for whoever has fallen into the trap to refuse. I know of cases where the criminal gang began with little gifts for the official's birthday, then it followed with a little gift for his wife or children, and later with a little help when the official had to move to a new house or buy a new car and so on. In the end, the net becomes so tight that the only way out is to commit suicide. It has happened, sometimes.

The many national borders that drugs, people and arms must cross could not possibly be passed if a well-oiled system of corruption were not in place. Corruption is facilitated by government inefficiency, by nebulous legislation and by the lack of allegiance to the State in civil servants and the population at large.

23

I will now move on to the third part of my presentation: how to defeat organised crime and corruption. There are two key words here: organisation and confiscation.

Let us start with organisation. While crime is organised, law enforcement is disorganised. The major criminal organisations are essentially transnational, but the tools used by governments to control them are still essentially national.

Organised crime did not benefit from the free movement of goods, money and people. Rather, it benefited from the shortfalls of the globalisation process, which has not yet involved the values of responsible citizenship and the tools for their defence.

In Europe, for instance, we combat what is essentially one and the same organised crime with dozens of different penal codes.

Crime can beat us not only because it is organised, but also because we are disorganised and slow to take action. We should learn from crime: we need to be as well co-ordinated as crime and as fast as crime, if we wish to prevail over crime.

We cannot afford to lose any more time. We know that a series of meetings between the major criminal groups took place in Warsaw in 1991, Prague in 1992, Berlin in 1993 and in 1994 in the French town of Beaune; the last one with representatives of the Italo-American Gambino family and the crime bosses of Japan, Colombia, Russia and China. We run the very real risk that in the next few years a global criminal system will take shape, a sort of 'hard core' made up of the major criminal organisations.

The first step in organisation is information. The best way to co-ordinate action is to circulate as much information as possible in all democratic countries.

Fortunately, we are not starting from scratch. The fight against organised crime, which encompasses the struggle against corruption, has two parallel objectives. The first is to attack the criminals themselves; the second is to attack their accumulated wealth.

To achieve these objectives, we must begin to think of building an international anti-crime area. Co-operation would be eased if each country provided for a specific crime, namely the crime of 'participation in a criminal organisation'. International co-operation between police authorities, the judiciary and bank supervisory authorities should be improved in the case of an allegation of this specific crime.

To combat corruption effectively two conditions are necessary. Every country must punish its citizens who have been found guilty of corrupting a civil servant of a foreign country. In addition it is necessary to grant adequate indemnity—using the criminals' seized assets—to those who have suffered a loss by the act of corruption.

There is no need, therefore, to resort to special measures that are alien to the democratic traditions of our countries. The problem is how to mount an ordinary response at a supranational level, not how to invent extraordinary instruments to be adopted nationally.

Let us now look at confiscation. When I described the main features of organised crime I gave a figure for the overall turnover of these organisations. Remember that their estimated annual volume of business is 500 billion dollars.

We often wonder how men so coarse and violent can possibly manoeuvre such colossal amounts of money. In 1993, when I was the chairman of the Parliamentary Anti-Mafia Committee, I asked a state witness for information on the investments and money laundering techniques of his organisation. He replied by asking me: 'If you have any money to invest, what do you do?' I answered: 'I ask an expert for advice.' And he said: 'We too. And if the investment turns out to be good, then what do you do?' 'I go back to the expert' was my answer. 'We too. And if the investment turns out to be bad, what do you do?' I answered: 'I'll change expert, I'll go to someone else.' And he said: 'We too. But we kill the first expert, and we let the second one know about it. That is the difference between you and us'.

The attack against criminal accumulated wealth is the modern dimension of the fight against organised crime. Money in the hands of these criminal organisations is more dangerous than a kalashnikov. The point I am trying to make is that confiscating the assets of criminal organisations is as important as confiscating their weapons.

Action needs to be taken at three different levels: a) the seizure and confiscation of the assets accumulated by the criminals; b) the fight against money laundering; c) the use of confiscated assets for social purposes.

Regarding the first level, I would simply like to highlight the positive Italian experience. After definitive sentences were handed down, and the criminals could not prove where their possessions came from, their assets were confiscated.

In November 1998 the Home Office Working Group on Confiscation suggested the civil forfeiture, or 'in rem forfeiture', should be extended to cover all the assets which proceed from all forms of crime. In UK between 1987 and 1996 only 157 drug trafficking confiscation orders for £100,000 or more were made against a background of over 45,000 convictions for supply of drugs. It is clear that the majority of the major criminals have not been affected by this legislation.

The second level of action is money laundering. Experts have estimated that transnational organised crime needs to launder about one half of its criminal proceeds, which means that the amount of money that is laundered every year stands at around 250 billion dollars. This is money that sooner or later will enter into the circuit of legal business, at least in part. It is money that will strongly distort the workings of markets and fair competition.

Most countries have adopted co-ordinated policies against market distortion. But there are about 70 countries that do not adhere to or simply do not apply the international conventions in this field. In so doing they void the efforts of those countries that have adopted more stringent regulations. According to IMF experts around 51% of all international financial transfers are to off-shore centres. This money is not all black money, but it is all taken out of the legal market. However, if the global co-operation network is to function, there must not be any loopholes.

To avert this risk, all of the democratic countries must take tough measures vis-a-vis the off-shore centres. Most of these centres are accomplices of organised crime and organised corruption—and they know it. I believe that the time has come for concerted action to place an embargo on those countries.

In March, in his address to the House of Commons, Foreign Minister Cook offered full British citizenship to the inhabitants of the overseas territories, on the express condition that they adopt specific regulations to combat money laundering.

The third level of action is related to the use of the assets confiscated from the criminal organisations. The seizure and definitive confiscation of the wealth accumulated by organised crime is necessary to undermine its economic power. But it is equally important to use the confiscated wealth for social purposes, building schools, libraries, parks, social centres and government agencies.

So far, Italy has confiscated from the Mafia and assigned to social purpose assets amounting to 117 billion lire (39 million pounds). This shows that legality does not mean law enforcement alone. It shows our citizens that the rule of law enables individual communities to win back what organised crime had taken away from them with violence.

Herbert Hart, in his considerations on law enforcement, said that the voluntary co-operation of citizens and their respect for the law are the essential requirements for the very existence of coercive power.

* * *

This brings me to the last part of my paper: how to educate people to respect the law, both in schools and in the business world.

In schools we must teach the younger generations that loyalty to civic values is as important in life as excellent professional training. In Italy we have started an awareness programme in schools, of the dangers surrounding corruption and the mafia and the benefit of honesty. Between 1994 and 1998, 800,000 children participated in this process.

As to the business community, we must dispel the fears of businessmen that controls on the legality of commercial or financial transactions may foreshadow forms of State control over the economy. In fact, this control helps to protect the businessmen and financial dealers who operate legally. If we let organised crime impose its products and enter the market the legal economy will be brought to its knees.

If we wish to ensure that the rule of law may be effective in combatting organised crime and corruption, both now and in the future, then we must broaden the scope of our action well beyond mere law enforcement. We must ensure that a culture based on the rule of law and the values of good citizenship becomes more ingrained in our society.

ECONOMIC CONVERGENCE AND EMU

by

PROF. DR. DR. H.C. HANS TIETMAYER

A lecture delivered at
the Sheldonian Theatre, Oxford,
on 3 June 1999

First of all, I should like to express my sincere gratitude for honouring me with your invitation. I am delighted and indeed honoured to be here, and to meet at the same time some good old friends and of course congratulate the 750th anniversary of the foundation of University College, Oxford. My own university was clearly a younger one—only 200 years old—but I have to add that my secondary school is a little bit older than the university here in Oxford as we have already celebrated its 1200th anniversary.

Oxford: the university, its colleges and facilities stand, on the one hand, for achievement and competitiveness in the modern world and, on the other, for history, tradition and heritage.

They are part of Britain's history and part of its future. And that means—I would quite expressly like to add—that they are also part of Europe's history and its future. Great Britain and Europe are not separate, mutually independent entities—either economically or culturally.

That leads me straightaway to the subject of Europe and its future.

I am naturally aware that this country is in the middle of a major process of clarification. How does it perceive its future position in Europe? How can it influence future developments in Europe? And, not least, what are the conditions of, and prospects for, future entry into monetary union?

Like many others in Europe, I am following this process with keen interest. And I have the impression that this debate in the United Kingdom has made significant progress over the past two years.

Of course, it is ultimately only the British themselves who can decide how they wish to shape their relations with Europe and European integration.

Even so, I do not wish to conceal the fact that I have a great deal of sympathy with the idea of the United Kingdom playing a crucial role in the future development of Europe and of it bringing not only its great traditions but also its criticism and especially its economic performance to bear in a constructive role in Europe and, hopefully, one day also into monetary union.

But that is a prospect on which the United Kingdom—its government, its parliament and its people—must take its own sovereign decision.

I do not presume to be able to offer you advice on that matter.

Instead, what I would like to do today is to draw your attention, in particular, to those aspects of monetary union which have played— and, in some cases, are still playing—a major role in our debate in Germany.

There will probably be very little of this that is really new to you. However, it might be valuable for you to know the points on which particular emphasis was—and is still being—placed in the German debate. Perhaps there will be some aspects which might provide a stimulating talking point for your own discussion.

* * *

Let me start with a simple, but fundamental, analysis:

What does monetary union really mean? What kind of environment does it create?

It seems to me that it possesses three essential characteristics:

Firstly: Membership of monetary union implies relinquishing monetary sovereignty. Monetary policy becomes European. Naturally enough, that concerns the level of the official interest rates. But it goes further than that. European monetary policy includes the framework in which monetary policy is conducted, embracing not only its structure and the way in which the central banking system perceives its own role, but also the strategy and instruments used, as well as much else besides.

Secondly: the monetary union is designed to last. Entry into it is a road on which there is no turning back. In monetary union, a 'trial marriage' is no longer possible, and that is different to the ERM or European Monetary System. Reversing that decision could entail incalculable economic and political costs. No one ought to place any faith in that being a realistic option.

And thirdly: the euro area is unlike every other currency area which is defined—at least usually—by the area of a single sovereign nation state. There is a single monetary policy for the euro area. However the other areas of policy, such as budget, tax and social policies, are still largely decentralised. Fiscal policy, in particular, must abide by the rules set down in the Maastricht Treaty and in the supplementary stability and Growth Pact.

These three fundamental characteristics appear straightforward and self-evident. But they have important implications:

One key implication is that the euro area requires lasting economic convergence—convergence in the sense that each single country must be able to keep up with the others on a permanent common currency basis, without recourse to national monetary policy or changes in the exchange rate.

That necessity of lasting convergence has to be seen against the backdrop of unrestricted capital movements and supranational monetary policy.

A traditional nation state with its own currency has several options available for fostering convergence within its own currency area. There are largely uniform economic and taxation policies to prevent excessive deviations in politically-induced conditions for investment. There is a national budgetary policy which can give financial support to regions which are lagging behind the general trend. And there is a largely similar and similarly funded system of welfare.

These are all things which the euro area does not have at a supranational level—or, at least, not to anything like the same extent.

There are some—mainly on the continent—who regret this because it means that economic convergence cannot be created, at least, actively promoted by a centralised policy.

Others—and I suspect that the overwhelming majority of the British people belong to this camp—believe this to be a good thing.

Europe should not be a dominant centralised entity, nor should it have an egalitarian public-sector system of adjustment. It should be decentralised, organised on the principles of subsidiarity and geared to competition.

Your Prime Minister put this in a nutshell: 'Integrate where necessary. Decentralise where possible.' I would add that I have a great deal of sympathy for that position.

However, one also has to see the other side of the coin. One problem remains: how can a politically decentralised monetary union safeguard the necessary lasting convergence of all its member states?

Ultimately, there is only one way of doing this. Safeguarding lasting convergence in a politically decentralised monetary union must rest on two pillars.

- firstly, on each country's own sustained competitiveness and on each country's own efforts;
- and, secondly, on a fundamental willingness to accept certain binding rules and abide by them on permanent basis.

That is the only way in which a monetary union with a decentralised political structure can succeed—not only economically, but also politically: in other words, without excessive conflict among the participating countries.

* * *

The competitiveness of each single country is obviously initially one economic condition for a kind of optimum currency area.

Basically, an optimum currency area means that, in the longer term, there is no need for adjustment of the nominal exchange rate because other adjustment mechanisms are effective, say, as a result of internal flexibility or a high degree of labour mobility.

That is clear in theory. In practice, there is a fundamental problem: how can the ability to 'keep up' be assessed? And how is it possible to safeguard that ability and the willingness to utilise it on a lasting basis?

Now, in some way or another, the track record and the basic situation in the countries concerned have to be taken into account.

The Maastricht Treaty does that and stipulates convergence criteria for that purpose. These may not have been the final pearl of wisdom in the strict economic sense, but that should not make us overlook what fundamental pillars the convergence criteria represent in terms of the logic of a politically decentralised currency union.

I am aware of the fact that we Germans, by insisting on a strict interpretation of those criteria, have not always been given a good press internationally in the past. It may also be the case that the debate in Germany did not always take the best possible course, especially when somewhat too much emphasis was being placed on the decimal place in the budgetary policy of the test year, for example.

But the key element—taking the convergence criteria seriously—was,

34

and still is, correct. The criteria were, and remain, a test of ability and political will, at least at the time of entry.

Basic conditions for passing a test are undoubtedly the abilities to keep the internal value of the currency stable and to maintain the exchange rate with our partners without tensions—an exchange rate, moreover, which is determined *a priori* as a central rate, not one which is defined at a later stage in the moment of entry itself. For that reason, the Treaty calls—and, in our opinion unquestionably calls—for a two-year membership in ERM without tensions.

In this interpretation of convergence—which has determined the German debate—there are two ideas which play a key role:

- the idea of the permanence of sufficient convergence;
- and the idea that the present and the past are a test of the future ability to stay the pace on a lasting basis.

Perhaps you feel the debate in Germany has a different emphasis from the one here.

In the United Kingdom, convergence is sometimes understood more in the sense of convergence in the business cycle.

By no means do I wish to disparage that. Naturally enough, I am aware of the current economic background in the United Kingdom.

And we do already have this problem in the euro area at the moment. The cyclical position of Ireland, for instance, is obviously different from that in most countries on the continent.

There can be no question at all: if a country believes that it is in its own longer-term interest to enter, it will look for a time which it feels to be opportune. That is no more than an act of human reason.

I would only like to point out that what we have here is a case of the debate being weighted somewhat differently. And, naturally, one has to perceive the backdrop to this: in other words, the fact that the tie which is created is a permanent one. It is not least for this reason that it is right for the British government, in particular, to place repeated stress on the subject of internal flexibility.

I believe that there is unanimity in the debate both in the United Kingdom and in Germany that economic convergence does not imply uniformity.

Firstly: it does not imply uniform structures. It is true that competition—precisely in a monetary union—exerts pressure to find efficient solutions, but they do not have to be the same everywhere. Even in monetary union, there will still be room for different economic traditions and styles. However, the competitiveness of all the participating economies must be ensured on an enduring basis.

Secondly: convergence does not imply uniform policies in all areas. On the contrary: besides the central decision making for monetary policy, a decentralised monetary union calls on national policy to exercise its own responsibility for maintaining or creating competitive economic structures. In key areas, too, powers can indeed remain with the nation states. Nevertheless, individual approaches, say in the area of taxes, must not lead to distortions on the markets.

Thirdly: convergence least of all implies uniform living conditions or equal prosperity in all the participating countries and regions. It may very well be that the way in which the single market and the single currency work will assist less well-developed regions that face up resolutely to competition in catching up quickly and sustainably. But that must happen on the basis of competition. There can be no *a priori* guarantee of that.

* * *

Lasting economic convergence based primarily on market forces is one fundamental precondition for a politically decentralised monetary union.

The second fundamental precondition is that the participating countries agree binding rules for certain areas and are prepared to abide by them on an enduring basis.

There are rules of this kind—in addition to the general rules for the single market—principally for budgetary policy, where it has a particular direct relevance to the financial markets.

Some of the rules for budgetary policy are:

Firstly, the central banks must not finance the public budgets.

Secondly, there is a no-bail-out-clause. The Community is not liable or the commitments of individual member states.

Thirdly, the governments have committed themselves to avoiding excessive deficits and excessive stocks of debt, and, where they exist, to reducing them immediately.

Fourthly, in normal circumstances the deficit should be close to balance.

These rules are not undisputed. Some ask whether the no-bail-out clause is not sufficient. Is the reference to the inherent responsibility of national budgetary policy not enough on its own?

In my view, these objections put matters too simply.

Firstly, we do not know under what financial market conditions a financial crisis in one EMU country might break out. (To be honest, I hope that is something we shall never learn.) However, we can tell from the recent national financial crises in other regions that systemic risk can easily arise. Or, at least, the argument is advanced that there is the possibility of systemic risk—and who would want to let it come to that? Of course, the markets are aware of that, too. For that reason, there is always likely to be a certain problem of credibility with regard to the no-bail-out clause.

Secondly, it is true that a single currency does not imply the same long-term interest rates for all issuers. Certainly not. The quality of the borrowers and liquidity aspects also play a role. But, naturally, for the foreign exchange risk is shared equally by all the participating countries. For that reason alone, there exists an interdependence among the participating countries.

And there naturally also exists an interdependence in macroeconomic terms. If the budgets of individual participating countries—especially the large ones—have excessive recourse to the capital markets, this will obviously be a burden on the other countries.

An excessive government deficit eats up private savings. That is a factor which either uses up internal capital resources and/or has an impact on the euro's external relations—quite apart from an overburdening of monetary policy as a result of an excessively expansionary fiscal policy.

For these reasons, there is undoubted justification not only for a no-bail-out clause but also for defining limits for the national budget deficit and for the general government debt ratio.

I wish that the national budgetary policymakers in the participating countries would perceive these rules not merely as a constraint but also as an opportunity of pursuing a rational policy on a sustained basis.

One thing is clear, of course: setting the rules is not enough. The rules also have to be accepted by the countries involved. And they have to be enforced if the need arises. That is not an easy matter, as we learnt only last week in Brussels.

* * *

The second area in which rules are set is within the framework of monetary policy.

One of the key elements of monetary union, as provided for in the Maastricht Treaty is, without doubt, the independence of the European Central Bank and of the participating national central banks: in other words, the independence of the Eurosystem.

The economic rationale for a central bank which is independent of the instructions and influence of political bodies is rooted in the finding that it is generally easier for such a central bank to keep the value of the currency stable on a lasting basis.

That higher degree of monetary stability benefits the economy and society in various ways.

It increases planning certainty in the economy, which fosters a culture of long-termism. It makes it easier for enterprises to fund investment decisions in the longer term. That generally results in a stronger long-term orientation in economic decision making. Incidentally, that was one of the key considerations when your new government gave greater autonomy to the Bank of England two years ago.

A stable currency is, at the same time, an element of social policy. It is often precisely those who are not so well off in economic terms who find it difficult—or impossible—to protect themselves against inflation or inflationary developments.

Finally, money which has a stable value is also a factor of political philosophy. Confidence in the currency is, to some extent, confidence in the state and its institutions.

That is, at least, the case in Germany, partly owing to our experience of two galloping inflations in the first half of this century, but also partly on account of the ideas of economists such as Alfred Müller-Armack and Ludwig Erhard, who introduced into German economic policy the leitmotif of the social market economy, with a stable currency as one key element.

This economic rationale has now resulted in a trend towards greater central bank independence outside of Europe as well. That is perhaps also one factor—among others—which helps to explain the high degree of price stability that prevails worldwide at present.

One fundamental objection to central bank independence raises the question of democratic legitimacy.

Is a central bank which is independent of political instructions and influence in keeping with a democracy?

I believe that there are two preconditions which have to be fulfilled for an independent central bank to be unquestionably compatible with a democratic system.

Firstly: the assigning of independence and the mandate has to have been arrived at democratically, or at the least, by virtue of an implicit consensus, and on an explicit foundation provided either by law, a constitution or by a treaty—like that of Maastricht—to which the parliaments have given their consent.

Secondly: the mandate of the independent central bank must be unambiguous.

Political value judgements among various competing aims may be made only by those who have acquired direct democratic legitimacy as a result of elections. It is precisely for that purpose that elections give a mandate.

The decision-making body of an independent central bank, which is not elected directly, may not make any autonomous value judgements among various competing aims. An overriding objective has to be specified in advance.

That is precisely what the Maastricht Treaty does. It specifies the primary objective of price stability.

Hence, the independent central bank remains anchored in the democratic structure of the state.

In my view, the limitedness of the central bank's mandate is thus a corollary of its political, democratic and constitutional legitimacy.

For that reason alone, I believe that broadening the mandate would lead to problems for the European System of Central Banks. That applies, for example, to the idea of extending the scope of the central bank's mandate beyond price stability to include growth and full employment as additional objectives. That is quite apart from the fact that I do not perceive any trade-off between those aims—at least in the longer term.

Assigning other tasks can also cause difficulties for an independent central bank, however. Assigning sole responsibility for banking supervision or a lender-of-last-resort function, for instance, may give rise to difficulties.

Such a plurality of mandates might give rise to a situation in which the independent ECB has to choose among different objectives, say between the objective of stable prices, on the one hand, and the consolidation of individual financial institutions, on the other. Fundamentally, that would be a political value judgement. If a financial institution has to be bailed out, then it has to be done on budgetary decisions; that means that the public sector has to provide the necessary money. Therefore, caution—at least—should be exercised in terms of delegating additional tasks to the ECB.

In addition to those two basic preconditions—the democratic assignment of tasks and an unambiguous mandate—tying the independent central bank into a democratic system naturally requires something more: it calls for transparency and accountability.

Independent monetary policy cannot and must not be remote from the general public.

In saying that, it is essential to distinguish precisely what is meant by transparency.

Does transparency mean full disclosure of the deliberations, arguments and motives behind a decision: in other words, transparency of the *situation* in which a decision is taken?

Or does transparency principally aim at disclosure of the *discussion process* by which is a decision is made?

In terms of the transparency of the overall *situation* in which a decision is taken, the ECB endeavours to do this by a comprehensive disclosure of its judgements and the assessments which determine its decisions. Of course, I do not rule out the possibility of improvement in one respect or another. It is not yet even six months that the ECB has borne responsibility for monetary policy. We are therefore all still involved in the learning process.

Incidentally, I personally would have nothing against also identifying arguments pointing to a decision other than the one that was ultimately taken but which happened to be rejected after taking other arguments into account.

Transparency concerning the internal *process* of consultation and decision-making is another matter, however.

I regard that as problematic since it may ultimately imperil the efficiency of monetary policy decision-making. Why?

Firstly, it puts the frankness and confidentiality of the discussion at risk. It can, at least, lead to confidential discussions being shifted to other circles. And that undermines the unity of the decision-making body.

Secondly, it may endanger the credibility and standing of individual members, who are open to argument and, on account of new insights, may alter their position during the discussion process.

I therefore feel that this second approach to greater public transparency is not without problems, besides the question of whether the minutes that are published are really in line with what happened or whether they are really painting another picture. And I also have doubts as to whether it really introduces more clarity and calculability in monetary policy for the markets. Of course some market places want to have that, because it is best to have such a position and then take it to make money out of that, because of course traders want to have changes and want to have special points where they can then do their transactions, but this is not the reason for having more transparency.

I admit that my reservations also have to do with the idea that the decision-making body should have a feeling of collective responsibility. And that also includes the attempt to seek an internal consensus and demonstrate it externally.

Now, it may be that some people find the desire to seek consensus stuffy and old-fashioned. In the final analysis, I believe it is not.

Allow me to make a few remarks in this connection: I come from a central bank which—together with its predecessor institution, the Bank deutscher Länder—has been independent for over 50 years.

During that period, it was necessary to fend off several attacks from the political field. In saying that, it has to be borne in mind that a simple parliamentary majority would have sufficed for a legislative amendment to remove the Bundesbank's independence.

In situations of conflict, an independent central bank needs the support of as broad a segment of public opinion as possible. That will also be the case for the ECB, even though its independence is anchored in the Maastricht Treaty.

But to be given that support, a central bank needs more than just a good record over the longer term. What is also important is that it can demonstrate a minimum degree of unanimity.

That applies anyway in the event of a conflict. In that situation, if the central bank gives disparate signals to the outside world, the general public does not know at all what it is actually supposed to be supporting. Admittedly, it is comparatively easy to create unanimity in the event of a conflict.

But the central bank's standing with the general public, which is intended to be a protection in the event of a conflict—that is something which it has to have earned and built up beforehand.

And it has the standing only if the general public is aware of what the central bank stands for. If the general public asks what the bank's standpoint is, it wants a clear-cut answer and not a response enumerating the various possibilities of position 1, position 2, position 3 and so on.

A central bank must be identifiable by its basic stance. That can scarcely be achieved without a minimum of collective awareness.

I fully understand the objection that this must not lead to individual responsibility becoming lost in the decision-making bodies There is something in that.

I wish, however, that critics who have never had to withstand a serious attack on the independence of the central bank would have somewhat more respect for the concepts of consensus and unanimity.

* * *

Finally, allow me to indulge in a reflection of a fundamental nature.

We are certainly all in agreement that the euro has to be a success. And that is a permanent challenge.

Whether the euro becomes a success story is something on which it is impossible to make a final judgement after less than six months. The euro certainly has a great potential. Recent exchange rate movements have not altered that fact.

Clearly, the decline in the euro's external value over the last few days has not been good news.

We shall study developments carefully.

Yesterday the Governing Council of the ECB had a serious discussion on that point. We came to the following conclusion which was presented to the press after the meeting by President Duisenberg.

> 'The euro is a currency firmly based on internal price stability and therefore has a clear potential for a stronger external value. Since that start of Stage Three of EMU the euro has become the second most important international currency in the world, and the policy of the Eurosystem will safeguard its internal purchasing power, thereby also supporting the international role of the euro.'

But in making a reasonable assessment of the opportunities and risks inherent in the project of monetary union, we shall maintain a longer-term perspective.

In the eyes of future generations, the ultimate test of the success of monetary union will one day consist of three questions:

- Has monetary union been able to safeguard lasting monetary stability? And that means internationally.
- Have the participating economies coped with the conditions of monetary union? And that means avoiding conflict.
- And: has the euro brought the people and peoples of Europe closer together?

The answers to those questions have a lot to do with convergence,

43

although not only with economic convergence in the narrow sense of parallel trends in the hard data on productivity, labour costs, or whatever.

It also has much to do with convergence in values, in beliefs and in aims. That is something which cannot be measured mathematically, but is it nevertheless important.

I feel that it is precisely this convergence in thinking which has increased over the past few years between the United Kingdom and Germany, with both sides having learnt from each other.

That is not intended to be a sixth test for your entry into monetary union, but no harm can come from it either.

THE UNIVERSE IN A NUTSHELL

By

PROF. STEPHEN HAWKING CH CBE FRS

A lecture delivered at
Oxford Town Hall
on 25 October 1999

I have been asked to say a little about myself, what I have achieved, and what obstacles I have had to overcome. I think my greatest achievement is being alive today. In 1963, I was diagnosed as having ALS, or motor neurone disease, and told I had two or three years to live. Or rather, that is what my parents were told. I wasn't told anything, not even the name of my condition. But I could tell it was pretty bad, and I didn't want to hear the details.

Before I was diagnosed with ALS, I was very laid back, and bored with life. But the prospect of an early death concentrated my mind wonderfully. I realised that life was good, and that there was a great deal I wanted to do. My condition developed much less rapidly than anyone had expected, and, fortunately, it did not interfere with my great interest, which was understanding how the universe works. I won't describe my scientific career, except to say I think I can feel satisfied with what I have achieved, particularly given that my expectations had been reduced to zero. I can safely say that I'm happier now than I was before my condition appeared.

I have also been asked what other career I might have followed. In fact, my ALS ruled out most careers apart from theoretical physics. But before it developed, I had toyed with the idea of being a political leader. I might have been the Prime Minister. However, I'm glad I left the job to Tony. I think I probably get more job satisfaction than he does. And my work is likely to last longer.

To get back to why we are here, I will now give my lecture.

Hamlet said, 'I could be bounded in a nutshell, and count myself a King of infinite space'. I think what he meant was that although we humans are very limited physically, particularly in my own case, our minds are free to explore the whole universe, and to boldly go where even Star Trek fears to tread.

But is the universe actually infinite or just very large. And is it everlasting or just long lived. How could our finite minds comprehend an infinite Universe. Isn't it pretentious of us even to make the attempt?

At the risk of incurring the fate of Prometheus, who stole fire from the ancient Gods for human use, I believe we can, and should, try and understand the universe. As I shall describe in this talk, we have already made remarkable progress in understanding the Cosmos, particularly in the last few years. We don't yet have a complete picture, but I think that may not be far off.

47

The most obvious thing about space, is that it goes on and on and on. We don't expect the universe to end in a brick wall, though there's no logical reason why it couldn't. But modern instruments like the Hubble space telescope allow us to probe deep into space.

What we see is billions and billions of galaxies, of various shapes and sizes. There are giant elliptical galaxies and spiral galaxies like our own. Each galaxy contains billions and billions of stars, many of which will have planets round them. Our own galaxy blocks our view in certain directions, but one can plot the positions of all the galaxies and the cone of directions, with us at the point of the cone at the centre.

The galaxies are distributed roughly uniformly throughout space, with some local concentrations and voids. The density of galaxies appears to drop off at very large distances, but that seems to be because they are so far away and faint that we can't make them out. As far as we can tell, the universe goes on in space forever, much the same as it is here.

Although the universe seems to be much the same at each position in space, it is definitely changing in time. This was not realised until the early years of this century. Up to then, it was thought the universe was essentially constant in time. It might have existed for an infinite time, but that seemed to lead to absurd conclusions. If stars had been radiating for an infinite time, they would have heated up the universe to their temperature.

Even at night, the whole sky would be as bright as the Sun, because every line of sight would have ended either on a star, or a cloud of dust that had been heated up, until it was as hot as the stars. So the observation that you have all made, that the sky at night is dark, is very important. It implies that the universe cannot have existed for ever, in the state we see today. Something must have happened in the past to make the stars turn on a finite time ago. Then the light from very distant stars wouldn't have had time to reach us yet. This would explain why the sky at night isn't glowing in every direction.

If the stars had just been sitting there forever, why did they suddenly light up a few billion years ago. What was the clock that told them it was time to shine. This puzzled those philosophers, like Immanuel Kant, who believed that the universe had existed forever. But for most people, it was consistent with the idea that the universe had been created, much as it is now, only a few thousand years ago.

However, discrepancies with this idea began to appear, with

observations by the hundred inch telescope on Mount Wilson, in the 1920s.

First of all, Edwin Hubble discovered that many faint patches of light, called nebulae, were in fact other galaxies, vast collections of stars like our Sun, but at a great distance. In order for them to appear so small and faint, the distances had to be so great that light from them would have taken millions or even billions of years to reach us. This indicated that the beginning of the universe couldn't have been just a few thousand years ago.

But the second thing Hubble discovered was even more remarkable. By an analysis of the light from other galaxies, Hubble was able to measure whether they were moving towards us, or away. To his great surprise, he found they were nearly all moving away. Moreover, the further they were from us, the faster they were moving away. In other words, the universe is expanding. Galaxies are moving away from each other.

The discovery of the expansion of the universe was one of the great intellectual revolutions of the 20th century. It came as a total surprise and it completely changed the discussion of the origin of the universe. If the galaxies are moving apart, they must have been closer together in the past. From the present rate of expansion, we can estimate that they must have been very close together indeed about ten to fifteen billion years ago.

But maybe the galaxies fell towards each other, just missed colliding and then moved away from each other, like we see them moving apart today. This idea that there hadn't been a beginning to the universe seemed to be supported by the work of two Russians, Lifshitz and Khalatnikov, and became almost an article of faith in the Soviet Union. The fact that it avoided the awkward question of the creation of the universe was an obvious attraction.

In fact, I began my research in cosmology just about the time that Lifshitz and Khalatnikov published their conclusion that the universe didn't have a beginning. I realised that this was a very important question, but I wasn't convinced by the arguments that Lifshitz and Khalatnikov had used.

Instead, Roger Penrose and I managed to prove geometrical theorems to show that the universe must have had a beginning, if Einstein's General Theory of Relativity was correct, and certain reasonable conditions were satisfied. It is difficult to argue with a mathematical theorem, so in the end Lifshitz and Khalatnikov conceded that the universe should have a beginning. Although the idea of a beginning to the universe might not be very welcome to communist ideas, ideology was never allowed to stand in the way of science in physics, unlike biology. Physics was needed for the bomb, and it was important that it worked.

We are used to the idea that events are caused by earlier events, which in turn are caused by still earlier events. There is a chain of causality stretching back into the past. But suppose this chain has a beginning, suppose there was a first event. What caused it? This was not a question that many scientists wanted to address. They tried to avoid it, either by claiming like the Russians that the universe didn't have a beginning. Or they maintained that the origin of the universe did not lie within the realm of science, but belonged to metaphysics or religion.

In my opinion, this is not a position any true scientist should take. If the laws of science are suspended at the beginning of the universe, might not they also fail at other times?

A law is not a law if it only holds sometimes. I believe that we should try to understand the beginning of the universe on the basis of science. It may be a task beyond our powers, but at least we should make the attempt.

The geometrical theorems that Roger Penrose and I proved showed that the universe must have had a beginning, but didn't give much information about the nature of that beginning. They indicated that the universe began in a Big Bang, a point where the whole universe, and every thing in it, were scrunched up into a single point of infinite density. At this point, Einstein's General Theory of Relativity would have broken down. Thus, one cannot use it to predict in what manner the universe began. One is left with the origin of the universe, apparently being beyond the scope of science.

This was not a conclusion that I, or a number of other people, were happy with. The reason Einstein's General Relativity broke down near the Big Bang was that it was what is called a classical theory. That is, it implicitly assumed what seems obvious from common sense, that each particle had a well-defined position and a well defined speed.

In such a so called classical theory, if one knew the positions and speeds of all the particles in the universe at one time, one could calculate what they would be at any other time in the past or future. However, in the early 20th century, scientists discovered that they couldn't calculate exactly what would happen on very short distances. It wasn't just that they needed better theories. There seems to be a certain level of randomness or uncertainty in nature that cannot be removed however good our theories.

It can be summed up in the Uncertainty Principle, which was formulated in 1925 by the German scientist, Werner Heisenberg. One cannot accurately predict both the position, and the speed, of a particle. The more accurately the position is predicted, the less accurately you will be able to predict the speed, and vice versa.

Einstein objected strongly to the idea that the universe is governed by chance. His feelings were summed up in this dictum, God does not play dice. But all the evidence is that God is quite a gambler. The universe is like a giant casino, with dice being rolled, or wheels being spun, on every occasion.

A casino owner risks losing money each time dice are thrown, or the roulette wheel is spun. But over a large number of bets, the odds average out and the casino owner makes sure they average out in his or her favour. That is why casino owners are so rich. The only chance you have of winning against them is to stake all your money on a few rolls of the dice, or spins of the wheel.

It is the same with the universe. When the universe is big, there are a very large number of rolls of the dice, and the results average out to something one can predict. But when the universe is very small, near the Big Bang, there are only a small number of rolls of the dice, and the Uncertainty Principle is very important.

In order to understand the origin of the universe, one therefore has to incorporate the Uncertainty Principle, into Einstein's General Theory of Relativity. This has been the great challenge in theoretical physics in the last thirty years. We haven't solved it yet, but we have made a lot of progress, and we feel we may be close.

Because the universe keeps on rolling the dice, to see what happens next, it doesn't have just a single history, as one might have thought. Instead, the universe must have every possible history, each with its own probability.

There must be a history of the universe, in which Oxford United won the Cup, though maybe the probability is low. This idea that the universe has multiple histories may sound like science fiction, but it is now accepted as science fact. It is due to Richard Feynman, who worked at the eminently respectable California Institute of Technology, and played the bongo drums in a strip joint up the road.

Scientists are now working to combine Einstein's General Theory of Relativity and Feynman's idea of multiple histories, into a complete unified theory, that will describe everything that happens in the universe. This unified theory will enable us to calculate how the universe will evolve, if we know its state at one time. But the unified theory will not in itself tell us how the universe began, or what its initial state was.

For that, we need what are called boundary conditions, things that tell us what happens on the frontiers of the universe, the edges of space and time. But if the frontier of the universe was just at a normal point of space and time, we could go past it and claim the territory beyond as part of the universe.

On the other hand, if the boundary of the universe was at a jagged edge where space and time were scrunched up and the density was infinite, it would be very difficult to define meaningful boundary conditions.

However, Jim Hartle of the University of California, Santa Barbara, and I realised there was a third possibility. Maybe the universe has no boundary in space and time. At first sight, this seems to be in direct contradiction with the geometrical theorems that I mentioned earlier. These show that the universe must have had a beginning, a boundary in time. However, there is another kind of time, called imaginary time that is at right angles to the ordinary real time, that we feel going by.

One can follow the history of the universe in imaginary time and it is very different from the history in real time. In particular, the history of the universe in imaginary time need have no beginning or end. Imaginary time behaves just like another direction in space.

Thus the histories of the universe in imaginary time can be thought of as the curved space of the universe, changing in the imaginary time direction. The histories can therefore be regarded as curved surfaces, in the space and imaginary time directions.

If they were curved like a saddle, or if they were flat, they would go off to infinity and one would have the problem of specifying what the boundary conditions were at infinity. But one can avoid having to specify boundary conditions at all, if the histories of the universe in imaginary time are closed surfaces, like the surface of the Earth.

The surface of the Earth doesn't have any boundaries or edges. I know, because I have been round the world, and I didn't fall off. I even went to Antarctica, to check there wasn't an edge there.

If the histories of the universe in imaginary time are indeed closed surfaces, as Jim Hartle and I proposed, it would mean the universe is entirely self contained. It doesn't receive any input from the outside, telling it what it should be like. Instead, everything in the universe would be determined by the laws of science and by rolls of the dice within the universe. This may sound presumptuous, but it is what I and many other scientists believe.

As I said earlier, even if the boundary condition of the universe is that it has no boundary, it won't have just a single history. Instead, the histories in imaginary time will correspond to every possible closed surface. Each history in imaginary time will determine a history in real time. Thus we have a super abundance of histories for the universe. What picks out the particular history, or set of histories that we live in, from the set of all possible histories of the universe?

One point that we can notice is that many of these possible histories of the universe won't go through the sequence of forming galaxies and stars that was essential to our own development. It may be that intelligent beings can evolve without galaxies and stars, but it seems unlikely. Thus the very fact that we exist as beings that can ask the question, Why is the universe the way it is, is a restriction on the history we live in. It implies it is one of the minority of histories that have galaxies and stars.

This is an example of what is called the Anthropic Principle. The Anthropic Principle, says that the universe has to be more or less as we see it, because if it were different, there wouldn't be anyone here to observe it.

Many scientists dislike the Anthropic Principle, because it seems rather hand waving, and not to have much predictive power. But the Anthropic Principle can be given a precise formulation and it seems to be essential, when dealing with the origin of the universe. M theory, which is our best candidate for a complete unified theory, allows a very large number of possible histories for the universe. Most of these histories are quite unsuitable for the development of intelligent life.

Either they are empty or too short lasting, or too highly curved, or wrong in some other way.

Yet according to Richard Feynman's multiple histories idea, these uninhabited histories can have quite a high probability.

We really don't care how many histories there may be that don't contain intelligent beings. We are interested only in the subset of histories in which intelligent life develops. This intelligent life need not be anything like humans. Little green men would do as well. In fact, they might do rather better. The human race does not have a very good record of intelligent behaviour.

As an example of the power of the Anthropic Principle, consider the number of directions in space. It is a matter of common experience that we live in three-dimensional space. That is to say, we can represent the position of a point in space by three numbers, for example, latitude, longitude and height above sea level. But why is space three-dimensional. Why isn't it two, or four, or some other number of dimensions, like in science fiction?

In fact in M theory, space has ten dimensions, but it is thought that seven of the directions, are curled up very small, leaving three directions, that are large and nearly flat.

It is like a drinking straw. The surface of a straw is two-dimensional. However, one direction is curled up into a small circle, so that from a distance the straw looks like a one-dimensional line.

Why don't we live in a history in which eight of the dimensions are curled up small, leaving only two dimensions that we notice?

A two dimensional animal would have a hard job digesting food. If it had a gut that went right through, like we have, it would divide the animal in two, and the poor creature would fall apart.

So two flat directions are not enough for anything as complicated as intelligent life. On the other hand, if there were four or more nearly flat directions, the gravitational force between two bodies would increase more rapidly as they approached each other. This would mean that planets would not have stable orbits about their Suns. They would either fall into the Sun, or escape to the outer darkness and cold.

Similarly, the orbits of electrons in atoms would not be stable, so matter,

Tony Blair: Toynbee Hall, London, 18 March 1999

Luciano Violante: All Souls College, Oxford, 1 June 1999

Hans Tietmeyer: Sheldonian Theatre, Oxford, 3 June 1999

Stephen Hawking: Oxford Town Hall, 25 October 1999

University College's
Builders of The Millennium
Lecture Series

Sir Richard Branson: Examination Schools, Oxford, 8 November 1999

Sir V.S. Naipaul: Examination Schools, Oxford, 11 November 1999

Rupert Murdoch: Sheldonian Theatre, Oxford, 1 December 1999

as we know it, would not exist. Thus although the multiple histories idea would allow any number of nearly flat directions, only histories with three flat directions will contain intelligent beings. Only in such histories will the question be asked, why does space have three dimensions.

A three-dimensional universe evolving in imaginary time will be represented by four dimensional curved surface. That is to say, each event in the history of the universe can be labelled by four numbers. Three numbers label the position in space, and the fourth is the imaginary time of the event. The simplest closed four-dimensional surface is a round sphere, like the surface of the Earth, but with two more dimensions.

This history in imaginary time determines a history of the universe in the real time that we experience. In this, the universe is the same at every point of space, and it is expanding in time. In these respects, it is like the universe we live in. But the rate of expansion is very rapid, and it keeps on getting faster. Such accelerating expansion is called inflation, because it is like the way prices go up and up, at an ever-increasing rate.

Inflation in prices is generally held to be a bad thing but in the case of the universe inflation is very beneficial. The large amount of expansion smooths out any lumps and bumps there may have been in the early universe. As the universe expands, it borrows energy from the gravitational field to create more matter. The positive matter energy is exactly balanced by the negative gravitational energy, so the total energy is zero.

When the universe doubles in size, the matter and gravitational energies both double. So twice zero is still zero. If only the financial world were so simple.

If the history of the universe in imaginary time were a perfectly round sphere, the corresponding history in real time would be a universe that continued to expand in an inflationary manner for ever. While the universe is inflating, matter could not fall together to form galaxies and stars, and life, let alone intelligent life like us, could not develop. Thus although histories of the universe in imaginary time that are perfectly round spheres are allowed by the multiple histories idea, they are not of much interest.

However, histories in imaginary time that are slightly flattened at the north pole are much more relevant. The corresponding history in real time will expand in an accelerated, inflationary manner at first. But then the expansion will begin to slow down and galaxies can form. In order for intelligent life to be able to develop, the flattening at the north pole must be very slight. This will mean that the universe will expand by an enormous amount.

The record of monetary inflation occurred in Germany between the Wars, when prices rose billions of times. But the amount of inflation that must have occurred in the universe is at least a billion billion billion. Of course, that was before the present government tackled inflation.

Because of the Uncertainty Principle, there won't be just one history of the universe. Instead, the histories in imaginary time will be a whole family of slightly deformed spheres, each of which corresponds to a history in real time that inflates for a long time, but not indefinitely. We can then ask which of these allowable histories is the most probable. It turns out that the most probable histories are not completely smooth, but have tiny ups and downs.

When I say tiny, I really mean tiny. The departures from smoothness are of the order of one part in a hundred thousand. Nevertheless, although they are so small, we have managed to observe them, as small variations in the microwaves that come to us from different directions in space.

In a map of the sky in microwaves, made by the Cosmic Background Explorer satellite, the different colours indicate different temperatures. But the whole range from red to blue is only about a ten thousandth of a degree. Yet this is enough variation between different regions of the early universe for some of them to stop expanding and to collapse again under their own gravity to form galaxies and stars. So such maps are the blue print for all the structure in the universe.

What will be the future behaviour of the most probable histories of the universe. There seem to be various possibilities, which are compatible with the appearance of intelligent beings. They depend on the amount of matter in the universe. If there is more than a certain critical amount, the gravitational attraction between the galaxies will slow them down and will eventually stop them flying apart.

They will then start falling towards each other and will all come together in a Big Crunch that will be the end of the history of the universe in real time. When I was in the Far East, I was asked not to mention the Big Crunch, because of the effect it might have on the market. But the markets crashed, so maybe the story got out somehow. In this country people don't seem too worried about a possible end, twenty billion years in the future. You can do quite a lot of eating, drinking and being merry, before that.

If the density of the universe is below the critical value, gravity is too weak to stop the galaxies flying apart forever. All the stars will burn out and the universe will get emptier and emptier, and colder and colder. So again, things will come to an end, but in a less dramatic way. Still, we have a few billion years in hand. As well as matter, the universe may contain what is called vacuum energy, energy that is present even in apparently empty space.

By Einstein's famous equation, $E = mc^2$, this vacuum energy has mass. This means that it has a gravitational effect on the expansion of the universe. But remarkably enough the effect of vacuum energy, is the opposite of that of matter. Matter causes the expansion to slow down, and can eventually stop and reverse it. On the other hand, vacuum energy causes the expansion to accelerate, like in inflation. We can therefore try to determine the amounts of matter and vacuum energy in the universe, from various observations.

One can show the results in a diagram in which the matter density is the horizontal direction, and vacuum energy is the vertical direction. The dotted line shows the boundary of the region, in which intelligent life could develop. If the matter density and vacuum energy lie outside this region, galaxies wouldn't have formed, and we wouldn't be here to ask what the matter and vacuum energy were. Observations of supernovas indicate that the values probably lie in the elliptical region coloured red. Observations of how much matter is clustered suggest the values lie in the blue region. And observations of the microwaves from space indicate that the values lie in the purple region.

Fortunately, all three regions have a common intersection. If the matter density and vacuum energy lie in this intersection, it means that the expansion of the universe has begun to speed up again, after a long period of slowing down. Despite what politicians may tell you, we have not seen the end of inflation. It seems that inflation may be a law of nature.

In this lecture, I have tried to explain how the behaviour of the vast universe can be understood in terms of its history in imaginary time.

This is a tiny, slightly flattened sphere. So it is quite like the nutshell with which I began the lecture. Yet this nut encodes everything that happens in real time. So Hamlet was quite right. We could be bounded in a nut shell, and count ourselves Kings of infinite space.

What more can I say after that. Thank you for listening.

ENTERPRISE IN THE NEW MILLENNIUM

By

SIR RICHARD BRANSON

A lecture delivered at
the Examination Schools, Oxford,
on 8 November 1999

[*Sir Richard Branson's lecture differed from the others in the series in comprising a shorter lecture, and a more extensive question and answer session. Only his introductory speech is published here.*]

I thank you very much, and I'm delighted and honoured to be here. I have some good news and I have some bad news. First the good news: there has never been a more exciting time to better build an economy. The Internet is opening up new territory faster than the Californian Gold Rush; capital is now available for people with greater ideas and talents; and government is committed to free enterprise and encouraging risk-taking. Now the bad news: statistically here in Britain people with high IQ's and Oxbridge degrees are more likely to be the accountants and lawyers than the entrepreneurs. And I suppose that I'm one of those statistics. I never finished school—I wasn't much good at it anyway—and this is the first time I've ever been to university. Yet I would like to think that Virgin is one of the more enterprising companies of the millennium and hopefully the next.

So what makes Virgin enterprising, and how can we possibly benefit from the lessons that I have spent a lifetime and several millions of pounds and a few grey hairs to learn? Well, it's not the Internet. The Internet is important, but its real impact is as just one part of a much bigger shift, the transfer of financial power from large companies and governments to individual consumers—you and me.

Virgin has never had a strategy in the sense that some MBA students would recognise it. We've never been big on focus groups or market research—focus groups rejected the Sony Walkman. We have simply followed our instincts as human beings, and as consumers, and so we have done naturally what other companies have paid consultants a lot of money to do. We have been consumer-focussed.

Little of this is driven by the Internet or e-commerce. Both have made it possible for small businesses to succeed in a global market, but neither are fundamentally changing the world. After all, the late 19th century had its own Victorian Internet, and the first transatlantic cable was not a product of the 1980s but rather the 1880s. Over a hundred years ago Harrods advertised its telegraphic address, and received orders and goods and services from all over the world, even to the extent that it had as much virtual trade as a percentage of its sales in 1899 as it does today.

One can take the analogy too far, but I'm sure you get the point. My personal view is that the biggest contribution the Internet is making is in reducing costs and giving people access to perfect information—the dream for a perfect economy, although that was so for the 19th century economists. Too many British entrepreneurs have become obsolete because they focussed on what they own—banks, shipping companies, airlines—and not on what their customers wanted. P & O was one of the largest international passenger carriers in the world, and because they decided to focus on their core business, shipping, they missed the opportunity to become the world's dominant airline. At Virgin we went to the other extreme: a record company that brought you the Sex Pistols ended up flying you off to the States.

So how far can any company safely stretch its brand name? Could the Sex Pistols Company sort out your banking needs? Initially we struggled with this idea—how could we do it differently? The answer was obvious: we had to start again. The most complicated, cumbersome and expensive way of managing your money is to spread it over a current account, credit card, savings account and mortgage. Why not have one account that you can use to do everything from paying the gas bill to buying a house? So that's what we did: we launched the Virgin Money Account just over a year ago. We've lent over a billion pounds to spawn a rash of competitors and we didn't do it on our own. We combined our brand with the capabilities of a 250-year old Scottish bank, the Royal Bank of Scotland contributing the infrastructure, the credit expertise and the backlog of service. We have become a virtual company. I firmly believe that within ten years the vast majority of successful companies around the world will have become virtual, and not only in the assets which they will use to provide services to customers.

This will mean that they can concentrate on better quality service and standards. These companies of the future will concentrate on one thing and one thing only—a personal relationship with all of us as a customer. The standards with which you and I are treated will be accountable to the brand name, but the company will have the freedom to establish legally binding contracts with all sorts of third party suppliers and shareholders, in order to make sure that you and I get the best quality at the lowest possible price.

Let me give you a couple of examples close to home. Later this week we are planning to launch the UK's first virtual mobile phone operator called Virgin Mobile. It will be the UK's fifth mobile phone network, but its entire operation is based upon the principles I have just mentioned. Virgin Mobile is outsourced for many business practices, with the exception of marketing and customer service. It is not building its own infrastructure to provide a service, but using one that has already been built by one of the foremost mobile phone companies in the market.

I believe that the virtual mobile network concept could be a serious threat to the current cellphone industry. The UK mobile industry is not so much the result of longer term planning by regulators or network operators as the outcome of misconceived industry rules which were drawn up in the early days of the mobile telephone. When Vodafone and Cellnet began services in 1985 they were unable to sell direct to consumers. Instead they were legally bound to sell through distributors. Even when those rules were changed, the net results were vertically implicated companies which had all expanded their fortune building their infrastructure and mimicking all of each other's business practices at every level. There should have been one set infrastructure with as many different operators using it as possible.

How will that be when from the consumer's point of view the net result has been incredibly complicated tariffs and over-expensive mobile usage equipment compared with the rest of Europe, despite the fact that we supposedly have much more competition? I think that you will find that when Virgin Mobile launches on Thursday we will be offering the simplest ever tariffs, and the best value for money products with the most innovative add-on services in the industry.

One of the key developments in the virtual world of business in the future will take place next March, when the British Government will be one of the first in the world to offer licences for a technology called Universal Mobile Telecommunications Service or UMTS as we call it. This new technology will turn your mobile phone into everything from a video conference or a miniature television through to a banking device, a credit card, and of course a boring old telephone. This will allow all of us in the future to literally carry around in our pocket the ability to make price comparisons instantaneously, to stay up to speed with events in real time, and, oh yes, even talk to each other.

Such models are rapidly going to be applied to every industry, in areas like the transport business, that will eventually aim that the so-called operator will become responsible only for the customer service and taking the flak when things go wrong. The planes, trains or buses and even private cars, will be owned, serviced, maintained and managed by those best able to do so, and the customer will get a cheaper and better quality of service as a result.

Now talking about taking flak when things go wrong, two and a half years ago we went into the rail business. We took a massive risk with the brand; we were taking on the West Coast main line, which had the oldest rolling stock and the most run-down infrastructure in the whole country. Well, when we won our franchise in 1997, we decided to take a completely different approach to the other operators. Instead of asking for a seven-year franchise, we asked for fifteen years. In return we said we would re-engineer the whole business and create a new one within five years. Well, three of those five years are up, and next month the world's most advanced train will be unveiled at a factory in Birmingham. It will be computer controlled, very comfortable and with all the latest electronic communications on board. It will also be the safest train ever used in the UK, and over the next two years fifty-three similar ones will operate and extremely fast service all over the county. The trains will be owned by the bank, and then taken by the manufacturers to the highest standards. In this future world Virgin will still be responsible for marketing, customer service and the selling of tickets. The whole project has raised four billion pounds of private money for both the new trains, the maintenance contracts and the upgrading of the track, to allow a doubling of the services—140 miles per hour—and a doubling of the number of trains every hour.

Although Virgin will not own any of these assets, it will operate them to the very highest standards, concentrating on what we are good at, while our partners concentrate on what they are good at—building and maintaining new state of the art trains.

One thing I believe Virgin stands for is a sense of challenge. We like to use the brand to take on some very large companies. We believe they exert too much power over the customer—the air industry, the financial services industry, the telephone companies and so on. However there are cases where a brand name has traditionally been almost synonymous with a product it is selling—Coca-Cola, Kelloggs and Hoover, for example—with heavy advertising and restrictive trade practices keeping it that way. In fact many American brand names like these grew up during the so-called era of the Robber Barons, which led to the introduction of America's excellent anti-trust laws in the early 20th century. At Virgin, we have a strategy of using the credibility of our brand to challenge the dominant players, in a range of industries where we believe the consumer is not getting value for money.

More recently another type of brand has developed. I'm sure that most of you have been intimate with a Mars bar at one time or other. It's a great product, and a great brand name, and they were wise enough not to try and use the same name for their very successful pet food business.

However, what I call the 'Mars syndrome' infects every marketing department and advertising agency in the country. They think that brands only relate to products where there is only a limited amount of stretch that is possible. They seem to have forgotten that no one has a problem playing a Yamaha piano, having ridden a Yamaha motorbike that day, or listening to Mitsubishi stereo in a Mitsubishi car driving past a Mitsubishi bank. This idea of brands crossing corporate structures and product areas, although rooted in British Victorian entrepreneurs' sense of destiny, has thus far found its modern manifestation in the Japanese management structure of Haritsu, where different businesses act as one family under one brand name.

I believe that there is almost no limit to what a brand can do, but only if used properly. We at Virgin are expanding and growing our use of the brand, but are always mindful of the fact that we should only risk on products and services that fit, or will fit, our very exacting criteria. That said, I believe that if you can run one company well, you can run virtually any company. Most importantly, because a company is only as good as its people, if you know how to motivate and deal with people, it doesn't matter whether you are taking on the airline industry, the soft drinks industry or the film industry, the same rules apply. But you should never go into an industry just with the purpose of making money. One has to passionately believe that it is possible to change the industry, to turn it on its head, to make sure it will never be the same again. With the right people, and that conviction, anything is possible. And you can then ignore those who go on about brand-stretching.

Since the airline's success, we have begun to evaluate prospective businesses by the five criteria that we think characterise the brand: the product or service must have, or have the prospect of becoming in the future, the best quality; it must be innovative; it must be good value for money; it must be challenging to existing alternatives; and it must have a sense of fun or cheekiness. We have found that people react much better to this than to the predictably straight propositions of many competitors, even in something as dry as financial services. If an idea satisfies at least four of these five criteria, we usually take a serious look at it, and in that way it's true to say that the core values of the brand are now playing a big role in dictating our entire business and corporate strategy.

Of course the flip side of enterprise in this virtual world of the future will be virtual crime. For those of you in the audience who do not want to spend the rest of your life working hard to build a real business, here is a ten-step guide to enterprising crime in the future:

1. Engage a top PR company to issue press releases every two weeks.
2. Set up a business with dot.com in the name.
3. Raise £100,000 from your friends, to back an extra ten million pounds.
4. And as the stock market flotation will take place within six months,
5. hire three LEA graduates to buy a printer-computer.
6. Get a dotcom website.
7. Raise two million pounds from venture capitalists and the bank gives up an extra twenty million.
8. Buy a real business for one million pounds, with two million pounds of revenues. Obtain press stories that claim that Investment banks now value your dotcom business for fifty million pounds, and refer to the hiring of ten MBA's to take your staff to over fifty people.
9. Sell off ten per cent of the company in the flotation valuing your company at a hundred million pounds.
10. Exit within in three years as disgracefully as the circumstances and the profits on the shares allow.

And a few people might think of doing this.

But seriously, there has never been a better time to chance the world legitimately. Take advantage of the privilege of being in a great institution like this, but don't let it shackle you. Trust your instincts and be prepared to have a go. And if everyone agrees that your idea won't work, prove them wrong. So you have two choices: let the world shape you, or you shape the world.

READING AND WRITING:
A PERSONAL ACCOUNT

By

Sir V.S. Naipaul

A lecture delivered at
the Examination Schools, Oxford,
on 11 November 1999

'I have no memory at all. That's one of the great defects of my mind: I keep on brooding over whatever interests me, by dint of examining it from different mental points of view I eventually see something new in it, and I alter its whole aspect. I point and extend the tubes of my glasses in all ways, or retract them.'

STENDHAL,
The Life of Henry Brulard

I was eleven, no more, when the wish came to me to be a writer; and then very soon it was a settled ambition. The early age is unusual, but I don't think extraordinary. I have heard that serious collectors, of books or pictures, can begin when they are very young; and recently, in India, I was told by a distinguished film director, Shyam Benegal, that he was six when he decided to make a life in cinema as a director.

With me, though, the ambition to be a writer was for many years a kind of sham. I liked to be given a fountain pen and a bottle of Waterman ink and new ruled exercise books (with margins), but I had no wish or need to write anything; and didn't write anything, not even letters: there was no one to write them to. I wasn't especially good at English composition at school; I didn't make up and tell stories at home. And though I liked new books as physical objects, I wasn't much of a reader. I liked a cheap, thick-paged children's book of Aesop's fables that I had been given; I liked a volume of Andersen's tales I had bought for myself with birthday money. But with other books, I had trouble. And that is, roughly, the thesis or theme of this talk, that because of one's background one had very much a trouble with reading. Literature is not after all the republic it might be assumed to be. And a similar kind of difficulty occurred when I became a writer. That is the argument I am going to ask you to follow.

For one or two periods a week at school—this was in the fifth standard—the headmaster, Mr. Worm, would read to us from *Twenty Thousand Leagues Under the Sea*, from the Collins Classics series. The fifth standard was the 'exhibition' class and was important to the reputation of the school. The exhibitions, given by the government, were for the island's secondary schools. To win an exhibition was to pay no secondary school fees at all and to get free books right through. It was also to win a kind of fame for oneself and one's school.

Our classroom was also Mr. Worm's office. He was an elderly mulatto, short and stout, correct in glasses and a suit, and quite a flogger when he roused himself, taking short, stressed breaths while he flogged, as though he were the sufferer. Sometimes, perhaps just to get away from the noisy little school building, where windows and doors were always open and classes were separated only by half-partitions, he would take us out to the dusty yard to the shade of the saman tree. His chair would be taken out for him, and he sat below the saman as he sat at his big desk in the classroom. We stood around him and tried to be still. He looked down at the little Collins Classic, oddly like a prayer book in his thick hands, and read Jules Verne like a man saying prayers.

Twenty Thousand Leagues Under the Sea wasn't an examination text. It was meant to give us 'background' and at the same time to be a break from our exhibition cramming; but those periods were periods of vacancy for us, and not easy to stand or sit through. I understood every word that was spoken, but I followed nothing. This sometimes happened to me in the cinema; but there I always enjoyed the idea of being at the cinema. From Mr. Worm's Jules Verne I took away nothing and, apart from the names of the submarine and its captain, have no memory of what was read for all those hours.

By this time, though, I had begun to have my own idea of what writing was. It was a private idea, and a curiously ennobling one, separate from school and separate from the disordered and disintegrating life of our Hindu extended family. That idea of writing—which was to give me the ambition to be a writer—had built up from the little things my father read to me from time to time.

My father was a self-educated man who had made himself a journalist. He read in his own way. At this time he was in his early thirties, and still learning. He read many books at once, finishing none, looking not for the story or the argument in any book but for the special qualities or character of the writer. He could savour writers only in little bursts. Sometimes he would call me to listen to two or three or four pages, seldom more, of writing he particularly enjoyed. He read and explained with zest and it was easy for me to like what he liked. In this unlikely way—considering the background: the racially mixed colonial school, the Asian inwardness at home—I had begun to put together an English literary anthology of my own.

These were some of the pieces that were in that anthology before I was twelve: some of the speeches in *Julius Caesar*; scattered pages from the early chapters of *Oliver Twist*, *Nicholas Nickleby* and *David Copperfield*; the Perseus story from *The Heroes* by Charles Kingsley; some pages from *The Mill on the Floss*; a romantic Malay tale of love and running away and death by Joseph Conrad; one or two of Lamb's *Tales from Shakespeare*; stories by O. Henry and Maupassant; a cynical page or two, about the Ganges and a religious festival, from *Jesting Pilate by* Aldous Huxley; something in the same vein from *Hindoo Holiday* by J.R. Ackerley; some pages by Somerset Maugham; some pages by Pearl Buck.

I was able to simplify everything I listened to. In my mind all the pieces (even those from *Julius Caesar*) took on aspects of the fairy tale, became a little like things by Andersen, far off and dateless, easy to play with mentally.

But when I went to the books themselves I found it hard to go beyond what had been read to me. What I already knew was magical; what I tried to read on my own was very far away. The language was too hard; I lost my way in social or historical detail. In the Conrad story the climate and vegetation was like what lay around me, but the Malays seemed extravagant, unreal, and I couldn't place them. When it came to the modern writers their stress on their own personalities shut me out: I couldn't pretend to be Maugham in London or Huxley or Ackerley in India.

I wished to be a writer. But together with the wish there had come the knowledge that the literature that had given me the wish came from another world, far away from our own.

* * *

We were an immigrant Asian community on a small plantation island in the New World. To me India seemed very far away, mythical, but we were at that time, in all the branches of our extended family, only about forty or fifty years out of India. We were still full of the instincts of people of the Gangetic plain, though year by year the colonial life around us was drawing us in. My own presence in Mr. Worm's class was part of that change. No one so young from our family had been to that school. Others were to follow me to the exhibition class, but I was the first.

Mangled bits of old India (very old, the India of nineteenth-century villages, which would have been like the India of earlier centuries) were still with me, not only in the enclosed life of our extended family, but also in what came to us sometimes from our community outside.

One of the first big public things I was taken to was the *Ramlila*, the pageant-play based on the *Ramayana*, the epic about the banishment

71

and later triumph of Rama, the Hindu hero-divinity. It was done in an open field in the middle of sugar cane, on the edge of our small country town. The male performers were barebacked and some carried long bows; they walked in a slow, stylised, rhythmic way, on their toes, and with high, quivering steps; when they made an exit they walked down a ramp that had been dug in the earth. The pageant ended with the burning of the big black effigy of the demon king of Lanka. This burning was one of the things people had come for; and the effigy, roughly made, with tar paper on a bamboo frame, had been standing in the open field all the time, as a promise of the event.

Everything in that *Ramlila* had been transported from India in the memories of people. And though as theatre it was crude, and there was much that I would have missed in the story, I believe I understood more and felt more than I had done during *The Prince and the Pauper* and *Sixty Glorious Years* at the local cinema. Those were the very first films I had seen, and I had never had an idea what I was watching. Whereas the *Ramlila* had given reality, and a lot of excitement, to what I had known of the *Ramayana*.

The *Ramayana* was the essential Hindu story. It was the more approachable of our two epics, and it lived among us the way epics lived. It had a strong and fast and rich narrative and, even with the divine machinery, the matter was very human. The characters and their motives could always be discussed; the epic was like a moral education for us all. Everyone around me would have known the story at least in outline; some people knew some of the actual verses. I didn't have to be taught it: the story of Rama's unjust banishment to the dangerous forest was like something I had always known.

It lay below the writing I was to get to know later in the city, the Andersen and Aesop I was to read on my own, and the things my father was to read to me.

* * *

The Island was small, 1,800 square miles, half a million people, but the population was very mixed and there were many separate worlds.

When my father got a job on the local paper we went to live in the city. It was only twelve miles away, but it was like going to another country. Our little rural Indian world, the disintegrating world of a remembered India, was left behind. I never returned to it; lost touch with the language; never saw another *Ramlila*.

72

In the city we were in a kind of limbo. There were few Indians there, and no one like us on the street. Though everything was very close, and houses were open to every kind of noise, and no one could really be private in his yard, we continued to live in our old enclosed way, mentally separate from the more colonial, more racially mixed life around us. There were respectable houses with verandas and hanging ferns. But there were also unfenced yards with three or four rotting little two-roomed wooden houses, like the city slave quarters of a hundred years before. Street life could be raucous: the big American base was just at the end of the street.

To arrive, after three years in the city, at Mr. Worm's exhibition class, cramming hard all the way, learning everything by heart, living with abstractions, having a grasp of very little, was like entering a cinema some time after the film had started and getting only scattered pointers to the story. It was like that for the twelve years I was to stay in the city before going to England. I never ceased to feel a stranger. I saw people of other groups only from the outside; school friendships were left behind at school or in the street. I had no proper understanding of where I was, and really never had the time to find out: all but nineteen months of those twelve years were spent in a blind, driven kind of colonial studying.

Very soon I got to know that there was a further world outside, of which our colonial world was only a shadow. This outer world— England principally, but also the United States and Canada—ruled us in every way: It sent us governors and everything else we lived by: the cheap preserved foods the island had needed since the slave days (smoked herring, salted cod, condensed milk, New Brunswick sardines in oil); the special medicines (Dodd's Kidney Pills, Dr. Sloan's Liniment, the tonic called Six Sixty-Six). It sent us—with a break during a bad year of the war, when we used the dimes and nickels of Canada—the coins of England, from the half-penny to the half-crown, and to these English coins we automatically gave values in our dollars and cents, one cent to a halfpenny, twenty-four cents to a shilling.

It sent us textbooks (Rivington's *Shilling Arithmetic*, Nesfield's *Grammar*) and question papers for the various school certificates. It sent us the films that fed our imaginative life, and *Life and Time*. It sent batches of *The Illustrated London News* to Mr. Worm's office. It sent us the Everyman's Library and Penguin Books and the Collins Classics. It sent us everything. It had given Mr. Worm Jules Verne. And, through my father, it had given me my private anthology of literature.

The books themselves I couldn't enter on my own. I didn't have the imaginative key. Such social knowledge as I had—a faint remembered village India and a mixed colonial world seen from the outside—didn't help with the literature of the metropolis. I was two worlds away.

I couldn't get on with English public-school stories (I remember the curiously titled *Sparrow in Search of Expulsion*, just arrived from England for Mr. Worm's little library). And later, when I was at the secondary school, I had the same trouble with the thrillers or adventure stories in the school library, the Buchan, the Sapper, the Sabatini, the Sax Rohmer, all given the pre-war dignity of leather binding, with the school crest stamped in gold on the front cover. I couldn't see the point of these artificial excitements, or the point of detective novels (a lot of reading, with a certain amount of misdirection, for a little bit of a puzzle). And when I tried plain English novels from the public library, too many questions got in the way—about the reality of the people, the artificiality of the narrative method, the purpose of the whole set-up thing, the end reward for me.

My private anthology, and my father's teaching, had given me a high idea of writing. And though I had started from a quite different corner, and was years away from understanding why I felt as I did, my attitude (as I was to discover) was like that of Joseph Conrad, himself at the time a just-published author, when he was sent the novel of a friend. The novel was clearly one of much plot; Conrad saw it not as a revelation of human hearts but as a fabrication of 'events which properly speaking are accidents only' 'All the charm, all the truth,' he wrote to the friend, 'are thrown away by the...mechanism (so to speak) of the story which makes it appear false.'

For Conrad, as for the narrator of *Under Western Eyes*, the discovery of every tale was a moral one. It was for me, too, without my knowing it. It was where the *Ramayana* and Aesop and Anderson and my private anthology (even the Maupassant and the O. Henry) had led me. When Conrad met H.G. Wells, who thought him too wordy, not giving the story straight, Conrad said, 'My dear Wells, what is this Love and Mr. Lewisham about? What is all this about Jane Austen? What is it all about?'

That was how I had felt in my secondary school, and for many years afterwards as well; but it had not occurred to me to say so. I didn't feel competent as a reader until I was twenty-five. I had by that time spent seven years in England, four of them here at Oxford, and I had a little of the social knowledge that was necessary for an understanding of

English and European fiction. I had also made myself a writer, and was able, therefore, to see writing from the other side. Until then I had read blindly, without judgment, not really knowing how made-up stories were to be assessed.

Certain undeniable things, though, had been added to my anthology during my time at the secondary school. The closest to me were my father's stories about the life of our community. I loved them as writing, as well as for the labour I had seen going into their making. They also anchored me in the world; without them I would have known nothing of our ancestry. And, through the enthusiasm of one teacher, there were three literary experiences in the sixth form: *Tartuffe*, which was like a frightening fairy tale, *Cyrano de Bergerac*, which for all its romanticism could call up the profoundest kind of emotion, and *Lazarillo de Tormes*, the mid-sixteenth-century Spanish picaresque story, the first of its kind, brisk and ironical, which took me into a world like the one I knew.

That was all. That was the stock of my reading at the end of my island education. I couldn't truly call myself a reader. I had never had the capacity to lose myself in a book; like my father, I could read only in little bits. My school essays weren't exceptional; they were only crammer's work. In spite of my father's example with his stories I hadn't begun to think in any concrete way about what I might write. Yet I continued to think of myself as a writer.

It was now less a true ambition than a form of self-esteem, a dream of release, an idea of nobility. My life, and the life of our section of our extended family, had always been unsettled. I was eaten up with anxiety. It was the emotion I felt I had always known.

* * *

The Colonial Government gave four scholarships a year to Higher School Certificate students who were at the top of their group. The question papers were sent out from England, and the students' scripts were sent back there to be marked. The scholarships were generous. They were meant to give a man or woman a profession. The scholarship winner could go at the government's expense to any university or place of higher education in the British Empire; and his scholarship could run for seven years. When I won my scholarship— after a labour that still hurts to think about: it was what all the years of cramming were meant to lead to—I decided only to go to Oxford and do the three-year English course. I didn't do this for the sake of Oxford and the English course; I knew little enough about either. I did it mainly to get away to the bigger world and give myself time to live up to my fantasy to become a writer.

To be a writer was to be a writer of novels and stories. That was how the ambition had come to me, through my anthology and my father's example, and that was where it had stayed. It was strange that I hadn't questioned this idea, since I had no taste for novels, hadn't felt the impulse (which children are said to feel) to make up stories, and nearly all my imaginative life during the long cramming years had been in the glorious cinema, and not in books. Sometimes when I thought of the writing blankness inside me I felt nervous; and then—it was like a belief in magic—I told myself that when the time came there would be no blankness and the books would get written.

At Oxford now, on that hard-earned scholarship, the time should have come. But the blankness was still there; and the very idea of fiction and the novel was puzzling me. A novel was something made up; that was almost its definition. At the same time it was expected to be true, to be drawn from life; so that part of the point of a novel came from half rejecting the fiction, or looking through it to a reality.

Later, when I had begun to identify my material and had begun to be a writer, working more or less intuitively, this ambiguity ceased to worry me. In 1955, the year of this breakthrough, I was able to understand Evelyn Waugh's definition of fiction (in the dedication to *Officers and Gentlemen*, published that year) as 'experience totally transformed'; I wouldn't have understood or believed the words the year before.

No magic happened in my three years here at Oxford, or in the fourth that the Colonial Office allowed me. I continued to fret over the idea of fiction as something made up. How far could the making up (Conrad's 'accidents') go? What was the logic and what was the value? I was led down many byways. I felt my writing personality as something very fluid that was grotesque. It gave me no pleasure to sit down at a table and pretend to write; I felt self-conscious and false.

If I had had even a little money, or the prospects of a fair job, it would have been easy then to let the writing idea drop. I saw it now only as a fantasy born out of childhood worry and ignorance, and it had become a burden. But there was no money. I had to hold on to the idea.

I was nearly destitute—I had perhaps six pounds—when I left Oxford, and that six pounds as I remember was given by University College for some piffling work I had done in the library as an act of charity before I went down. So that is all I had when I went to London to set up as a writer. All that remained of my scholarship, which seemed now to have been prodigally squandered, was the return fare home. For five months I was given shelter in a dark Paddington basement by an older cousin, a respecter of my ambition, himself very poor, studying law and working in a cigarette factory.

Nothing happened with my writing during those five months; nothing happened for five months afterward. And then one day, deep in my almost fixed depression, I began to see what my material might be: the city street from whose mixed life we had held aloof, and the country life before that, with the ways and manners of a remembered India. The material seemed easy and obvious when it had been found; but it had taken me four years to see it. Almost at the same time came the language, the tone, the voice for that material. It was as if voice and matter and form were part of one another.

Part of the voice was my father's, from his stories of the country life of our community. Part of it was from the anonymous *Lazarillo*, from mid-sixteenth-century Spain. (In my second year here at Oxford I had written to E.V. Rieu, editor of the Penguin Classics, offering to translate *Lazarillo*. He had replied very civilly, in his own hand, saying it would be a difficult book to do, and he didn't think it was a classic. I had nonetheless, during my blankness, as a substitute for writing, done a full translation.) And now I found that this mixed voice fitted. It was not absolutely my own when it first came to me, but I was not uneasy with it. And it was, in fact, the writing voice which I had been working hard to find. Soon it was familiar, the voice in my head. I could tell when it was right and when it was going off the rails.

To get started as a writer, I had had to go back to the beginning, and pick my way back—forgetting Oxford and London—to those early literary experiences, some of them not shared by anybody else, which had given me my own view of what lay about me.

* * *

In my fantasy of being a writer there had been no idea how I might actually go about writing a book. I suppose—I couldn't be sure—that there was a vague notion in the fantasy that once I had done the first the others would follow.

I found it wasn't like that. The material didn't permit it. In those early days every new book meant facing the old blankness again and going

77

back to the beginning. The later books came like the first, driven only by the wish to do a book, with an intuitive or innocent or desperate grasping at ideas and material without fully understanding where they might lead. Knowledge came with the writing. Each book took me to a deeper understanding and deeper feeling, and that led to a different way of writing. Every book was a stage in a process of finding out; it couldn't be repeated. My material at that time—my past, separated from me by place as well—was fixed and, like childhood itself, complete; it couldn't be added to. This way of writing consumed it. Within five years I had come to an end. My writing imagination was like a chalk-scrawled blackboard, wiped clean in stages, and at the end blank again, tabula rasa.

Fiction had taken me as far as it could go. There were certain things it couldn't deal with. It couldn't deal with my years in England; there was no social depth to the experience; it seemed more a matter for autobiography. And it couldn't deal with my growing knowledge of the wider world. Fiction, by its nature, functioning best within certain fixed social boundaries, seemed to be pushing me back to worlds—like the island world, or the world of my childhood—smaller than the one I now inhabited. Fiction, which had once liberated me and enlightened me, now seemed to be pushing me towards being simpler than I really was. For some years—three, perhaps four—I didn't know how to move; I was quite lost.

Nearly all my adult life had been spent in countries where I was a stranger. I couldn't as a writer go beyond that experience. To be true to that experience I had to write about people in that kind of position. I found ways of doing so; but I never ceased to feel it as a constraint. If I had had to depend only on the novel as a writing form I would probably have soon found myself without the means of going on, though I had trained myself in prose narrative and was full of curiosity about the world and people.

But there were other forms that met my need. Accident had fairly early on brought me a commission to travel in the former slave colonies of the Caribbean and the old Spanish Main. I had accepted for the sake of the travel; I hadn't thought much about the form.

I had an idea that the travel book was a glamorous interlude in the life of a serious writer. But the writers I had had in mind—and there could have been no others—were metropolitan people, Huxley, Lawrence, Waugh. I was not like them. They wrote at a time of empire; whatever their character at home, they inevitably in their travel became semi-imperial, using the accidents of travel to define their metropolitan personalities against a foreign background.

My travel that first time was not like that. I was a colonial travelling in New World plantation colonies which were like the one I had grown up in. To look, as a visitor, at other semiderelict communities in despoiled land, in the great romantic setting of the New World, was to see, as from a distance, what one's own community might have looked like. It was to be taken out of oneself and one's immediate circumstances—the material of fiction—and to have a new vision of what one had been born into, and to have an intimation of a sequence of historic events going far back.

I had trouble with the travel form. I didn't know how to travel for a book. I travelled as though I was on holiday, and then floundered, looking for the narrative. I had trouble with the 'I' of the travel writer; I thought that as traveller and narrator he was in unchallenged command and had to make big judgments.

For all its faults, the book, like the fiction books that had gone before, was for me an extension of knowledge and feeling. It wouldn't have been possible for me to unlearn what I had learned. Fiction, the exploration of one's immediate circumstances, had taken me a lot of the way. Travel, and the writing of a travel book had taken me further.

* * *

It was accident again that set me to doing another kind of nonfiction book. A publisher in the United States was doing a series for travellers, and asked me to do something about the colony. I though it would be a simple labour: a little local history, some personal memories, some word pictures.

I had thought, with a strange kind of innocence, that in our world all knowledge was easily available, that all history was stored somewhere and could be retrieved according to need. I found now that there was no local history to consult. There were only a few guidebooks in which certain legends were repeated. The colony had not been important; its past had disappeared. In some of the guidebooks the humorous point was made that the colony was a place where nothing of note had happened since Sir Walter Raleigh's visit in 1595.

I had to go to the records. There were the reports of travellers. There were the British official papers. In the British Museum there were very many big volumes of copies of relevant Spanish records, dug up by the

79

British government from the Spanish archives in the 1890s, at the time of the British Guiana-Venezuela border dispute. I looked in the records for people and their stories. It was the best way of organising the material, and it was the only way I knew to write. But it was hard work, picking through the papers, and using details from five or six or more documents to write a paragraph of narrative. The book which I had thought I would do in a few months took two hard years.

The records took me back almost to the discovery of my island; took me back almost to the time of Columbus. They showed me the aboriginal peoples, masters of sea and river, busy about their own affairs, possessing all the skills they had needed in past centuries, but helpless before the newcomers, and ground down over the next two hundred years to nonentity, alcoholism, missionary reserves and extinction. In this manmade wilderness then, in the late eighteenth century, the slave plantations were laid out, and the straight lines of the new Spanish town.

At school in the history class, slavery was only a word. One day in the schoolyard, in Mr. Worm's class, when there was some talk of the subject, I remember trying to give meaning to the word: looking up to the hills to the north of the city and thinking that those hills would once have been looked upon by people who were not free. The idea was too painful to hold on to.

The documents now, many years after that moment in the schoolyard, made that time of slavery real. They gave me glimpses of the life of the plantations. One plantation would have been very near the school; a street not far away still carried the Anglicised French name of the eighteenth-century owner. In the documents I went—and very often— to the city jail, where the principal business of the French jailer and his slave assistant was the punishing of slaves (the jailer's fees depended on the punishment given, and the planters paid), and where there were special hot cells, just below the roof shingles, for slaves who were thought to be sorcerers.

From the records of an unusual murder trial—one slave had killed another at a wake for a free woman of colour—I got an idea of the slave life of the streets in the 1790s, and understood that the kind of street we had lived on, and the kind of street life I had studied from a distance, were close to the streets and life of a hundred and fifty years before. That idea, of a history or an ancestry for the city street, was new to me. What I had known had seemed to me ordinary, unplanned, just there, with nothing like a past. But the past was there: in the schoolyard, in Mr.

Worm's class, below the saman tree, we stood perhaps on the site of Dominique Dert's Bel-Air estate, where in 1803 the slave *commandeur*, the estate driver or headman, out of a twisted love for his master, had tried to poison the other slaves.

More haunting than this was the thought of the vanished aborigines, on whose land and among whose spirits we all lived. The country town where I was born, and where in a clearing in the sugar cane I had seen our *Ramlila*, had an aboriginal name. One day in the British Museum I discovered—in a letter of 1625 from the king of Spain to the local governor—that it was the name of a troublesome small tribe of just over a thousand. In 1617 they had acted as river guides for English raiders. Eight years later—Spain had a long memory—the Spanish governor had assembled enough men to inflict some unspecified collective punishment on the tribe; and their name had disappeared from the records.

This was more than a fact about the aborigines. It to some extent altered my own past. I could no longer think of the *Ramlila* I had seen as a child as occurring at the very beginning of things. I had imaginatively to make room for people of another kind on the Ramlila ground. The practice of fiction by itself would not have taken me to this larger comprehension.

I didn't do a book like that again, working from documents alone. But the technique I had acquired—of looking through a multiplicity of impressions to a central human narrative—was something I took to the books of travel (or, more properly, inquiry) that I did over the next thirty years. So, as my world widened, beyond the immediate personal circumstances that bred fiction, and as my comprehension widened, the literary forms I practised flowed together and supported one another; and I couldn't say that one form was higher than another. The form depended on the material; the books were all part of the same process of understanding. It was what the writing career—at first only a child's fantasy, and then a more desperate wish to write stories—had committed me to.

The novel was an imported form. For the metropolitan writer it was only one aspect of self-knowledge. About it was a mass of other learning in the metropolis, other imaginative forms, other disciplines. For me, in the beginning, it was my all. Unlike the metropolitan writer I had no knowledge of a past. The past of our community ended, for most of us, with our grandfathers; beyond that we could not see. And the plantation colony, as the humorous guidebooks said, was a place where almost nothing had happened. So the fiction one did, about one's immediate circumstances, hung in a void, without a context, without the larger self-knowledge that was always implied in a metropolitan novel.

As a child trying to read, I had felt that two worlds separated me from the books that were offered to me at school and in the libraries: the childhood world of our remembered India, and the more colonial world of our city. I had thought that the difficulties had to do with the social and emotional disturbances of my childhood—that feeling of having entered the cinema long after the film had started—and that the difficulties would blow away as I got older. What I didn't know, even after I had written my early books of fiction, concerned only with story and people and getting to the end and mounting the jokes well, was that those two spheres of darkness had become my subject. Fiction, working its mysteries, by indirections finding directions out, had led me to my subject. But it couldn't take me all the way.

* * *

The second sphere of darkness was India. It was the greater hurt. It was a subject country. It was also the place from whose very great poverty our grandfathers had had to run away in the late nineteenth century. The two Indias were separate. The political India, of the freedom movement, had its great names. The other, more personal India was quite hidden; it vanished when memories faded. It wasn't an India we could read about. It wasn't Kipling's India, or E.M. Forster's, or Somerset Maugham's; and it was far from the somewhat stylish India of Nehru and Tagore.

It was to this personal India, and not the India of independence and its great names, that I went when the time came. I was full of nerves. But nothing had prepared me for the dereliction I saw. No other country I knew had so many layers of wretchedness, and few countries were as populous. I felt I was in a continent where, separate from the rest of the world, a mysterious calamity had occurred. Yet what was so overwhelming to me, so much in the foreground, was not be found in the modern-day writing I knew, Indian or English. In one Kipling story an Indian famine was a background to an English romance; but generally in both English and Indian writing the extraordinary distress of India, when acknowledged, was like something given, eternal, something to be read only as background. And there were, as always, those who though they could find a special spiritual quality in the special Indian distress.

I wrote a book, after having given up the idea. But I couldn't let go of the hurt. It took time—much writing, in many moods—to see beyond the dereliction. It took time to break through the bias and the fantasies of Indian political ideas about the Indian past. The independence struggle, the movement against the British, had obscured the calamities of India before the British. Evidence of those calamities lay on every side. But the independence movement was like religion; it didn't see what it didn't want to see.

For more than six hundred years after 1000 AD the Muslim invaders had ravaged the subcontinent at will. They had established kingdoms and empires and fought with one another. They had obliterated the temples of the local religions in the north; they had penetrated deep into the south and desecrated temples there.

For twentieth-century Indian nationalism those centuries of defeat were awkward. So history was rejigged; ruler and ruled before the British, conqueror and subject, believer and infidel, became one. In the face of the great British power, it made a kind of sense—to promote the idea of the wholeness of India before the British. But to promote that idea went against history. It went against the witness of a 14th century traveller like Ibn Battuta. He was a Moroccan and he wished to travel to all the countries of the Muslim world. Everywhere he went he lived on the bounty of the Muslim rulers, and he offered pure Arab piety in return.

He came to India as to a conquered Muslim land. He was granted the revenues (or crops) of five villages, and then—in spite of a famine—two more; and he stayed in the area of Delhi for seven years. In the end, though, he had to run. The Muslim ruler in Delhi, Ibn Battuta's ultimate patron, liked blood, daily executions (and torture) on the threshold of his hall of audience, with the bodies left lying for three days. Even Ibn Battuta, though used to the ways of Muslim despots the world over, began to take fright. When four guards were set to watch him he thought his time had come. He had been pestering the ruler and his officials for this and that, and complaining that the ruler's gifts were being soaked up by officials before they got to him. Now, with the inspiration of terror, he declared himself a penitent who had renounced the world. He did a full five-day fast, reading the Koran right through every day of his fast; and when he next appeared before the ruler he was dressed like a mendicant. The renunciation of the Moroccan theologian touched the hard heart of the ruler, reminded him of higher things, and Ibn Battuta was allowed to go.

In Ibn Battuta's narrative the local people were only obliquely seen.

They were serfs in the villages (the property of the ruler, part of the bounty that could be offered the traveller) or simple slaves (Ibn Battuta liked travelling with slave girls). The beliefs of these people had a quaint side but were otherwise of no interest to a Muslim theologian; in Delhi their idols had been literally overthrown. The land had ceased to belong to the local people and it had no sacredness for the foreign ruler.

In Ibn Battuta it was possible to see the beginnings of the great dereliction of India. To seventeenth-century European travellers like Thomas Roe and Bernier the general wretchedness of the people—living in huts outside the Mogul palaces—mocked the pretentiousness of the rulers. And for William Howard Russell, reporting in 1858 and 1859 on the Indian Mutiny for *The Times*, and travelling slowly from Calcutta to the Punjab, the land was everywhere in old ruin, with the half-starved ('hollow-thighed') common people, blindly going about their menial work, serving the British as they had served every previous ruler.

Even if I had never found words for it, I had believed as a child in the wholeness of India. The *Ramlila*—the pageant play based on the *Ramayana* that we saw performed in an open field just outside our little town—and our religious rites and all our private ways were part of that wholeness; it was something we had left behind. This new idea of the past, coming to me over the years, unravelled that romance, showed me that our ancestral civilisation—to which we had paid tribute in so many ways in our far-off colony, and had thought of as ancient and unbroken—had been as helpless before the Muslim invaders as the Mexicans and Peruvians were before the Spaniards; had been half destroyed.

* * *

For every kind of experience there is a proper form, and I do not see what kind of novel I could have written about India. Fiction works best in a confined moral and cultural area, where the rules are generally known; and in that confined area it deals best with things—emotions, impulses, moral anxieties—that would be unseizable or incomplete in other literary forms.

The experience I had had was particular to me. To do a novel about it would have been necessary to create someone like myself, someone of my ancestry and background, and to work out some business which would have taken this person to India. It would have been necessary more or less to duplicate the original experience, and it would have added nothing. The value of the experience lay in its particularity. I had to render it as faithfully as I could.

84

The metropolitan novel, so attractive, so apparently easy to imitate, comes with metropolitan assumptions about society: the availability of a wider learning, an idea of history, a concern with self-knowledge. Where those assumptions are wrong, where the wider learning is missing or imperfect, I am not sure whether the novel can offer more than the externals of things. The Japanese imported the novel form and added it to their own rich literary and historical traditions; there was no mismatch. But where, as in India, the past has been torn away, and history is unknown or unknowable or denied, I don't know whether the borrowed form of the novel can deliver more than a partial truth, a dim lighted window in a general darkness.

Forty to fifty years ago, when Indian writers were not so well considered, the writer R.K. Narayan was a comfort and example to those of us (I include my father and myself) who wished to write. Narayan wrote in English about Indian life. This is actually a difficult thing to do, and Narayan solved the problems by appearing to ignore them. He wrote lightly, directly, with little social explanation. His English was so personal and easy, so without English social associations, that there was no feeling of oddity; he always appeared to be writing from within his culture.

He wrote about people in a small town in South India: small people, big talk, small doings. That was where he began; that was where he was fifty years later. To some extent that reflected Narayan's own life. He never moved far from his origins. When I met him in London in 1961—he had been travelling, and was about to go back to India—he told me he needed to be back home, to do his walks (with an umbrella for the sun) and to be among his characters.

He truly possessed his world. It was complete and always there, waiting for him; and it was far enough away from the centre of things for outside disturbances to die down before they could get to it. Even the independence movement, in the heated 1930s and 1940s was far away, and the British presence was marked mainly by the names of buildings and places. This was an India that appeared to mock the vainglorious and went on in its own way.

These small people of Narayan's books, earning petty sums from petty jobs, and comforted and ruled by ritual, seem oddly insulated from history. On examination they don't appear to have an ancestry. They have only a father and perhaps a grandfather; they cannot reach back further into the past. They go to ancient temples; but they do not have the confidence of those ancient builders; they themselves can build nothing that will last.

Narayan spent part of his childhood in the state of Mysore. Mysore had a Hindu maharajah. The British put him on the throne after they had defeated the Muslim ruler at the end of the 18th century. The maharajah was of an illustrious family; his ancestors had been satraps of the last great Hindu kingdom of the south. That kingdom was defeated by the Muslims in 1565, and its enormous capital city (with all the accumulated human talent that had sustained it) almost totally destroyed, leaving a land so impoverished, so nearly without creative human resource, that it is hard now to see how a great empire could have arisen on that spot. The terrible ruins of the capital—still speaking four centuries later of loot and hate and blood and Hindu defeat, a whole world destroyed—were perhaps a day's journey from Mysore City.

Narayan's world is not, after all, as rooted and complete as it appears. His small people dream simply of what they think has gone before, but they are without personal ancestry; there is a great blank in their past. Their lives are small, as they have to be: this smallness is what has been allowed to come up in the ruins, with the simple new structures of British colonial order (school, road, bank, courts). In Narayan's books, when the history is known, there is less the life of a wise and enduring Hindu India than a celebration of the redeeming British peace.

So in India the borrowed form of the English or European novel, even when it has learned to deal with the externals of things, can sometimes miss their terrible essence. I too, as a writer of fiction, barely understanding my world—our family background, our migration, the curious half-remembered India in which we continued to live for a generation, Mr. Worm's school, my father's literary ambition—I too could begin only with the externals of things. To do more, as I soon had to, since I had no idea or illusion of a complete world always waiting for me somewhere, I had to find other ways.

TECHNOLOGY, DEMOGRAPHY AND OTHER HARD FACTS FACING THE BUILDERS OF THE MILLENNIUM

By

RUPERT MURDOCH AC

A lecture delivered at
the Sheldonian Theatre, Oxford,
on 1 December 1999

L ord Butler, lords, ladies and gentlemen. It is a great honour to be included in this splendid series of talks to commemorate the 750th anniversary of University College, and a great pleasure to return to the scene of my undergraduate days. But I fear that I may be here under false pretences.

For one think, unlike your opening speaker, the Prime Minister, or the brilliant Stephen Hawking, I would hardly classify myself as one of the 'builders of the millennium'. The evil media may try to make mere businessmen seem important, but we are really only minor facilitators in the game of shaping society.

For another, I am not certain that I can claim to fit comfortably into the great tradition of this wonderful College. As I understand it, William Beveridge was a prize Fellow here early in the century, and later, when Master, prepared the Beveridge report in the Master's lodgings. And such famous socialists as Clement Attlee, G.D.H. Cole and Harold Wilson were undergraduates or Fellows here.

Although it is true that when I was at Oxford I displayed a bust of Lenin in my rooms, I must confess that my later reflections have moved me somewhat away from the Attlee-Cole-Wilson School.

I do hope that journey does not disqualify me from contributing to this distinguished lecture series a few thoughts concerning opportunities and problems that confront those of you who will indeed be the builders of the next millennium.

Let me state at the outset that I count myself among the world's optimists. I believe that the opportunities we face are boundless, and that the problems that we face can be solved.

Thanks to advances in science and technology, and to related increases in the stock of human capital, the future before us is brighter than ever.

I am aware, of course, that there remain very significant areas of poverty in this world of plenty. But those are made by man, and can now be eliminated by man.

The only 'social exclusion' we will see in the coming millennium will be the result of wrong-headed government policies.

There are no major wars, thanks to the deterrent power of the arsenals of America and its democratic allies, most notably the United Kingdom.

True—we do have ugly ethnic and religious conflicts. But, with the unfortunate exception of those that rage in Africa, they do not threaten to wipe out entire generations of talented youngsters.

We have the ability to eliminate the physical threat of starvation. Technology now makes it possible for us to feed any foreseeable increase in the world's population.

We live in a world of surpluses, not scarcities. A world of six billion people, but one where we should be able to get those surpluses into the stomachs of the starving.

We no longer need fear running out of this or that resource: most raw materials are in ample supply to see us through centuries, and technology has proved its ability to come up with substitutes for just about anything nature is niggardly in providing.

We are rapidly learning how to cope with any of the environmental problems that we may face. The policies and the technology are already there—or soon will be—for the taking. Rising productivity and wealth will pay for them.

We have so improved living standards in most of the developed world that the poor of today live as well as the middle class of a relatively few years ago. And the developing world is moving fast to catch up.

I needn't recount here the advances that have changed the practice of medicine from one that at best could alleviate pain, but cure very few of our ailments, to one that is able to reconstruct or replace our body parts as they fail us due to disease or age.

After the imminent wave of bio-genetic medical breakthroughs is achieved, the maintenance or mechanical preservation of the brain will be the next great but achievable challenge.

These are bits of progress that I know about from reading newspapers—a practice I recommend to all of you. Equally, or perhaps more important, is the progress that I observe in my business life.

We have already entered an era of instant communication and the rapid diffusion of knowledge. This new era has come upon us with blinding speed.

A few short years ago people in Britain relied on two television channels for news and entertainment. Now they have scores of channels to choose from, both television and radio—or to ignore in favour of their PCs or video games.

And they will soon have hundreds of channels—very few of them owned by my company, no matter what you read in that portion of the press which for some strange reason seems so paranoid about any innovation.

A few short years ago telephony was a monopoly service made available slowly and at high cost only through wires. Fax machines were rare. And access to the Internet was reserved for a few.

Today, the telephone is becoming ubiquitous; wireless devices are competing with wired technology to provide service at constantly falling costs; fax machines are everywhere; and Internet access is growing so rapidly that firms that provide it are worth billions of pounds.

One fact in passing. After ten years the world has 400 million mobile phones. In five more, the number will be one billion, and within the lifetimes of most of us here, two or three billion. Which takes us to the most exciting aspect of all. The pace of change—rapid though it has been—is still accelerating.

Some experts say that over the long history of mankind 90% of the world's scientific progress and advances in living standards have been made in the last two hundred years.

I am not expert enough to say whether that is precisely true, but I suspect that it is. And I also suspect that in the relatively short period of the next twenty-thirty years we will see change at such a rapid rate as to equal that of the last two hundred.

It doesn't take a wild-eyed futurist to realise that our concept of the universe will change dramatically, and soon, as an increasingly educated population demands to know more and more about the world, or worlds, in which we all live, and as space exploration reveals new wonders to us.

So much of what was science fiction fifty years ago is today part of our lives. And we have every reason to expect that medical science will bless us with still much longer and more useful lives.

In my own business, change is so rapid that you take a holiday at your peril. You might return from even the shortest period of detachment from your business life to find a changed world.

Incumbency means less and less—and I suspect that is as true for politicians and for social elites as it is for businessmen.

By now you probably have noticed that I am not among those who fear that new technology will widen the gap between rich and poor. We are not headed for a world in which the rich will have access to computers and related technology, while the poor muddle along, computerless.

The new technologies are becoming widely available. First, the cost of computing is falling at a rapid rate. Second, the up-front costs of participating in this technological revolution are plummeting.

Moore's Law is alive and well. Gordon Moore, the founder of Intel, observed a striking trend almost thirty-five years ago—that each new memory chip contained roughly twice as much power as its predecessor—and each chip was released within eighteen months of the previous chip at half the cost. This pace of change continues to this very day.

The monumental consequence of this is that once-unimaginable processing power has been put into the hands of millions and millions of people.

Another rule of the computer age is Metcalfe's Law, which was developed by Bob Metcalfe of 3Com. Simply, to understand Metcalfe's Law, think of the humble telephone. What's a telephone worth to you—or its manufacturer—if there is only one other telephone, one other place to call? Not much, of course.

But their value increases geometrically based on the number of interconnections between devices. Once critical mass is reached the value of the network increases exponentially—far disproportionate to its physical growth.

And the mother of all history's interconnecting devices is, of course, provided by the computer and the Internet.

It is Metcalfe's Law which helps explain the sometimes mystifying valuation of the networks spawned within the Internet, such as Yahoo and AOL.

This recognition of the huge value offered by scale is why we are already seeing signs that it is in the interests of some businesses to give away computers, and in the perceived interest of still others to make access to the Internet free. Access to knowledge is becoming universal and free in every corner of the world. If not now, then very soon.

The model of free machines and free Internet access, made possible by selling advertising, is not far from the economic model of a broadsheet newspaper. With the notable exception of this nation's tabloids, newspapers derive a smaller portion of their revenue from the cover price; the bulk comes from what advertisers pay for access to the readers.

Indeed, we now have in London, and spreading elsewhere, daily newspapers that are free to readers, with advertisers bearing the total cost of putting out the paper. That is what some companies are now doing with computers and with Internet access. Only *The Times* is pressured by government authorities to charge more than it wishes.

Almost every innovation has seen businesses decide to swallow upfront costs in the hope of eventual recoupment. This is known as the razor and the blade business model—give away the razor to acquaint people with the advantages of the safety razor, and recover those costs by charging for the blades.

That was what happened in the case of cellphones, and that is what is happening in the case of digital television technology, and now in the case of computers.

So I can't agree with those who see new communications technology as a divisive social force. Quite the contrary. By facilitating communications between peoples of all nations, and of all income groups, it will help to bring people closer together.

You don't have to show your bank statement or a distinguished pedigree to deal yourself into a chat group on the Internet. And you don't have to be wealthy to e-mail someone on the far side of the globe.

And, thanks to modern technology, very soon you won't have to be a member of an elite to obtain higher education and all the benefits—pecuniary and non-pecuniary—that it confers. For new technology is forcing us to revise our concept of the university.

The World Bank estimates that there are now 70 million people in the world engaged in higher education, and that number will expand to at least 160 million by 2025.

Governments know that they cannot meet that demand in the traditional way—by building more and more schools and maintaining historic teacher-to-student ratios.

But they also know that unless they make education widely available their countries will be unable to compete in a knowledge-driven world economy.

The answer lies in the technology that allows students to study at the feet of great teachers, but from remote locations. Economies of scale are now available to our great teaching institutions.

Cyberspace networks are coming which will link universities, with students allowed to transfer credits among campuses and teachers available to thousands of students who will be educated in what we might call a Global Campus.

The great university that is sponsoring this lecture series, and distinguished architectural triumphs such as the building in which we now meet, will not become obsolete.

They and the teachers who inhabit them will, instead, become available and maybe even rich, by the miracle of modern technology to the millions who thirst for knowledge they can now be brought to them at reasonable cost.

Can something come between us and the world I have just sketched?— A world of rising living standards, increased education and human capital, longer and healthier lives, and cheaper and more widely available communication technology.

Certainly. For one thing, there will always be natural disasters. But even in the case of such calamities as earthquakes, technology is decreasing the destruction that results, and increasing our ability to find and assist survivors.

And there will always be unnatural disasters—those created by the mistaken policies of governments. Unfortunately, the danger that governments will blunder is a very real one. For their job will not be an easy one.

Change is not only accelerating; its direction and consequences are becoming less predictable. Central planning is a dangerous game.

I have a large stake in predicting where only one aspect of change—that in communications—will take us. And, I think, an able staff to advise me. But we still cannot with certainty see what the future holds.

There is no sense in screaming, 'Stop the world, I want to get off'. It won't stop, and we can't get off. Instead, we must accept the challenges that change presents, and grasp the opportunities that it creates.

As the Prime Minister has repeatedly pointed out, governments also must adapt to the changing world in which we live. And they must persuade their electorates that scientific and technological advances, and the changes that they bring, are not only irresistible, but good things.

The task that governments face will be complicated by the fact that their room for manoeuvre will be limited by some demographic and technological trends that are now emerging—most notably the fact that our populations are ageing.

As a consequence, fewer and fewer young workers will have to provide the tax base on which to erect pension and health systems to support a larger and larger number of retirees and pensioners. We have already passed the day in which the celebration of a one-hundredth birthday is worth much media coverage.

Now, I am not one of those who thinks that these demographic changes will inevitably produce declining living standards. Indeed, we should approach all of these demographic data with caution, as demographic trends have a way of reversing themselves with great suddenness. But even if we are faced with declining populations, I do not see that development as a major problem because:

First, productivity is increasing. And so long as the productivity of the work force increases, fewer workers can produce more and more goods and services, maintaining and increasing a society's standard of living, including the standard of living of non-working retirees.

Second, if any industrialised country wants more young workers it can easily get them—by importing immigrants. A nation's native-born population is not the only source of young workers. Immigrants may bring with them certain social problems, but they also bring young hands ready to work at particular jobs that the established native population is reluctant or lacking the skills to do—from emptying bedpans in hospitals, to writing computer programmes.

Third, and more important, the day is long past when a nation's strength was measured by the number of able-bodied men it could employ in its factories or deploy in trenches.

It is the *IQ* and *education* of the population, rather than its numbers, that determine the power and wealth of nations, and will continue to do so in the coming millennium.

Increasingly, human capital will be the key to a nation's prosperity. After all, only two percent of the value of a computer chip arises from the raw material it contains; 98% of the value represents the embodiment of human capital in that tiny chip.

Nobel laureate Gary Becker estimates that 75% of the capital of the United States is human capital.

I know that in my company what are traditionally thought of as 'assets'—bricks and mortar and desks and printing presses and computers—are worthless when compared to the people who use them, and who never appear on our balance sheet.

Which is why I feel that the Prime Minister's emphasis on improving educational standards is so well placed, even though I disagree with his view that central-government edicts rather than free parental choice is the best method of obtaining that objective.

So technology and empowerment of the individual can solve our educational problems. The problem of reforming the welfare state may prove less tractable.

Consider the question of health care, and the stubborn insistence of my generation on using the miracles of modern science and technology to live longer lives in a happier condition than we imagined possible only a few short years ago:

- hip and knee replacements have the elderly bounding around the tennis courts;
- quick and easy cataract operations enable them to enjoy books and television watching;
- heart surgery allows them to continue working or to have a vigorous retirement.

All of these and many more are now routine procedures, and all will certainly be supplemented by still further scientific advances that extend life and improve its quality.

The demand for these treatments will inexorably rise as science advances and the population ages; governments will be under huge pressure to make these treatments available to their citizens at far less than their cost.

But they will also find it increasingly difficult to raise and collect taxes.

We live in a world in which the high-earners that provide much of the revenues on which governments depend to finance their welfare and other programmes are increasingly mobile, and can more easily than ever be lured to countries with lower tax environments. Just look at the number of young Europeans working in London today.

Increased international mobility of executives, pop stars and university professors is not the only threat to nations' treasuries. There is also the Internet.

Let me cite just three examples:

- in this country, the Internet enables bettors to flee high taxes in Britain for lower ones in so-called tax havens—in the case of betting, that means Gibraltar;
- in America the Internet is making it increasingly difficult for state and local governments to collect sales taxes on items purchased over the wires and shipped to customers from other states;
- and how do you tax intellectual property, much of it software pulled from cyberspace that knows no taxing jurisdiction?

How, then, will the builders of the millennium cope with a world in which the tax-paying, young working population is shrinking relative to the service-demanding older population, at a time when the ability of governments to collect taxes will be under increasing threat?

I would suggest that mere tinkering with the existing welfare state will not solve the problem. Indeed, we probably have come full circle in this series, back to the opening speech of Prime Minister Blair. Recall that in that talk the Prime Minister called for radical reform of the system put in place in response to the Beveridge Report. He said:

'In the last 60 years the world has changed dramatically. It would

97

be surprising, lazy even, to believe that the solutions that suited a post-war Britain could work just as well in today's global economy'. So true.

True, too, was Mr. Blair's observation that 'Social justice is about mutual responsibility. It insists that we all accept duties as well as rights—to each other and to society...'

The first step in reforming the welfare state along the lines proposed by the Prime Minister has already been taken in both the US and the UK: those who can work must, and those who refuse to do so lose their claim on our compassion and the state's purse.

But even more fundamental steps must be taken to cope with the demographic trends I have described. The state can do just so much in caring for the elderly. The family must shoulder some of the burden.

But for that to happen, we must reverse the trends that have seen the family disintegrate before our very eyes. For it is only durable family values that can provide the sense of inter-generational obligation that will make the young tend to their elders, just as those, now elderly, once tended to them.

I know that it is now more voguish to speak of alternative life styles, and to argue that it is up to the individual to choose the lifestyle that best suits him or her. As one with strong libertarian leanings, I find that argument attractive—but not when the burden of supporting an alternative life style falls on society and the tax payer.

Studies here in Britain as well as in America prove conclusively that the incidences of child abuse, delinquency and poor school performance are all higher for children living in other than traditional family settings. The social costs of these problems are borne by all of us.

Worse still, as the population ages we will find that children reared in these settings will feel little responsibility for the parents who have done poorly by them.

In the words of that great historian, Gertrude Himmelfarb, in order to 'sustain those traditional values that encourage the individual to be virtuous', we need nothing short of a cultural renaissance. For which we cannot look to governments alone. We all have a part to play.

Clearly, we in the media make many mistakes. In part that is due to a dilemma that all of us in the media industries face. Our problem is whether it is right for us to tell the public that it is wrong to want what it wants, that the television programmes it wants to see are bad for it, and that we will combine to use our power to show them only what we believe they ought to see.

These are tough issues with which all in the media constantly wrestle; but broadly, I think we must trust the judgement of our customers—and fear the power of the off button which each of them commands.

In this age of ever-growing choice, the power of the viewer and the reader will go on growing in ways we cannot yet imagine.

No taste—no notion of quality—will need to go unmet. And the power of consumers to reject what we offer will be greater than ever.

Their judgement—as it always has been—will be swift to punish the media that misjudges public taste or morals, or the foreign media which fails to understand the sensibilities of host cultures.

And, as I have said, consumer choice is proliferating as we sit here. Which brings me back to the starting point of this lecture—the effect that the on-rush of technological change will have on our lives. Let me offer a generalisation for your consideration.

It is this: the Internet empowers the individual; it threatens the middleman with extinction; it threatens the entrenched; it threatens elites; this new technology will produce more direct scrutiny by citizens of their governments, and by consumers of companies that serve them.

Middlemen such as newspaper editors and TV producers will still be needed—but they will have to compete for attention against a host of new information providers, all of them suddenly allowed low-cost access to millions of consumers through the Internet.

There will be more information to distribute than can possibly make its way into print, or be absorbed by even the most skilled web browser—and there will be a need for editors to sort the relevant from the irrelevant, whether they deliver their product in the form of print or on the screen.

What I suspect will happen is that many publications will be able to establish themselves as reliable sources of information. That is, we will see the creation of new brands, and the extension of old, reliable brands to the Internet. Consumers burdened with too much choice will turn to the brands they trust, just as they do now with other consumer products.

But middlemen in the business of politics and news are not the only ones threatened by the empowerment of the individual.

In the field of finance, the advantage institutional investors once had in access to information is being eroded. 'Indeed, a reasonably experienced navigator of the world web could become as well informed as a top city fund manager with less than an hour's research', to quote *The Times*.

And we are seeing perhaps the most well paid of all middlemen, the investment banker, starting to face new offerings, made directly to potential investors by companies seeking to borrow money or raise equity capital at a fraction of the existing cost.

In the world of books, authors who once had to persuade middlemen to publish and distribute their books can now put their works on the web and invite the world to come and read.

I could also cite an unlimited number of examples of middleman-avoidance from the world of commerce. Automobile dealers in America are watching with horror as consumers trawl a variety of websites for price and performance information, and then place their orders for new vehicles directly onto the production lines with the touch of a computer key. So, too, with airline tickets. Search the web for the lowest fare, hit a button and pick up your boarding pass at the gate.

No middleman, in this case a travel agent, to come between you and a complete choice of fares and flights.

All of this adds up to one thing: empowerment of the individual. It was not so many years ago that Henry Ford provided the individual with the freedom of four wheels, personal mobility that liberated us from reliance on central planners who prefer transport systems that enable them to control the routes people travel and the times at which they do it. Get in your car, and go where you want to go when you want to go there.

Use public transportation, and you travel a route laid out by a bureaucrat, on a time schedule laid out by another bureaucrat. Little wonder that bureaucrats feel so threatened by the automobile that they would like to tax it out of existence—with the exception of course of their own limousines!

Now we are entering a new era of even greater individual empowerment. Its signs are everywhere. Traditionalists groan at the casual attire increasingly prevalent in the workplace. Why? Because it is a symbol of their loss of control over the individual, their inability to impose their standards on an increasingly educated, liberated and creative work force.

And governments—or at least some governments—groan at their inability to control entrepreneurs who want to put their capital where they, not some minister, think it will be most productive.

They groan that they cannot stop new technologies, new ideas, new cultural influences from crossing their borders. They worry that individuals will wrest so much power from governments as to make government less relevant.

These are foolhardy fears. For cultures and economies to flourish in the new millennium they must force themselves to open up to this changing world.

As I have argued, the change that can enrich our futures is the product of the IQs of empowered and creative individuals. And both logic and experience teach us that, whatever its imperfections, it is the American economic and social model of democratic government and free markets combined with a transparent legal system that maximizes individual creativity.

It has long been fashionable in Europe, and especially in France, to sneer at this so-called Anglo-Saxon model of free product markets and flexible human markets.

With America in the midst of an unprecedented economic expansion that has created jobs for everyone who wants to work, that has seen welfare rolls fall in half, and that has seen personal wealth soar, sneering becomes a bit less defensible.

After all, continental Europe has not created a single net new private sector job in twenty years, and is bedevilled by double-digit unemployment. Indeed, projections are that even the economic recovery now taking hold in France and Germany with their 15%

101

devaluation will be insufficient to bring the unemployment rates in those countries to anything like the low rates in Britain and America.

Prime Minister Blair and Chancellor Brown have noticed the contrast between the United States' economic success and Europe's faltering economies and, with a few unfortunate exceptions, are trying to move Britain as close to the U.S. entrepreneurial model as their party and their own social democratic instincts permit.

As you can see, I am of the view that governments will have to get out of the way of change. In short, they will have to know when to act and when to follow the advice of that much derided President, Ronald Reagan, who once advised a government colleague, 'Don't just do something, stand there.'

Good advice, I suggest, for over-eager government bureaucrats and regulators tempted to interfere with the creative builders of the new millennium, whomever they may turn out to be.

Many thanks for your attention.

EDITOR'S NOTE

The Editor wishes to thank all the contributors for their kind permission to have their lectures reprinted in this volume. In all cases, the texts supplied by the contributors have been checked against videotapes of the lectures as actually delivered, and the final versions have been edited accordingly.

The Editor would also like to thank Marion Hawtree, the Master's Secretary, for her help in typing the text on to disk, and Lord Butler and Biddy Hayward for their advice and assistance throughout the preparation of the book.